THE ULTIMATE GUIDE
TO THE
DARK KNIGHT

Dorling Kindersley

LONDON, NEW YORK, TORONTO,
MELBOURNE, MUNICH, and DELHI

Senior Editor Alastair Dougall
Senior Art Editor Gary Hyde
Designer Dan Bunyan
Publishing Manager Cynthia O'Neill
Art Director Cathy Tincknell
Production Nicola Torode
DTP Designer Jill Bunyan

First American Edition, 2001

03 04 05 06 10 9 8 7 6 5 4 3

Published in the United States by Dorling Kindersley Publishing Inc.,
375 Hudson Street, New York, New York 10014

Library of Congress Cataloging-in-Publication Data

Beatty, Scott, 1969-
    Batman : the ultimate guide to the dark knight / by Scott Beatty.--
1st American ed.
    p. cm.
    ISBN 0-7894-7865-X
    1. Batman (Comic strip)--Juvenile literature. 2. Batman (Fictitious
character)--Juvenile literature. [1. Batman (Comic strip) 2. Cartoons
and comics.]   I. Title.
  PN6728.B36 B533 2001
  741.5'973--dc21
                                    2001028441

Color reproduction by Media Development and Printing Ltd., UK

Printed and bound in Spain by Artes Gráficas Toledo S.A.U.
D.L. TO: 502-2003
Visit DC Comics online at www.dccomics.com or at keyword DC Comics on America Online.

Discover more at
www.dk.com

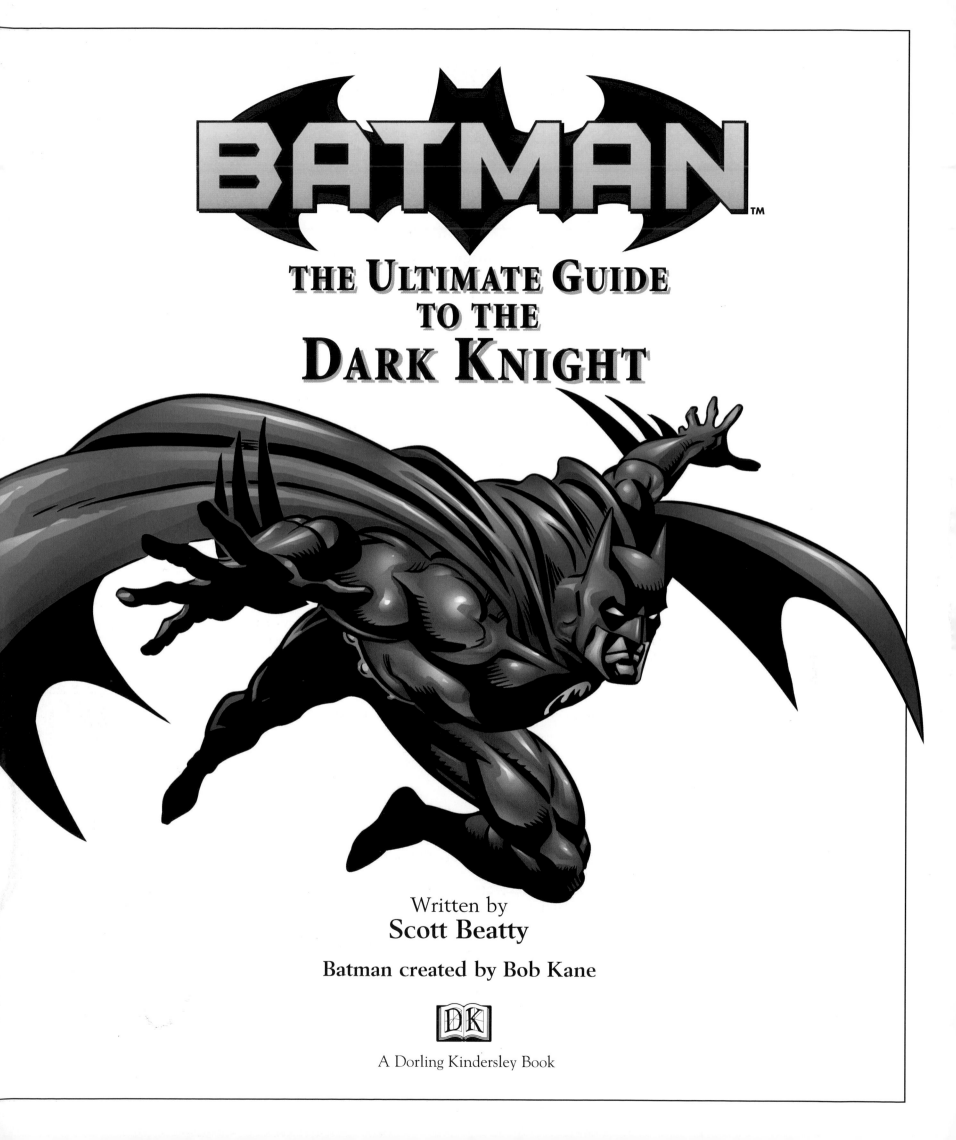

BATMAN™

THE ULTIMATE GUIDE TO THE Dark Knight

Written by
Scott Beatty

Batman created by Bob Kane

A Dorling Kindersley Book

CONTENTS

FOREWORD

HOW MANY OTHER FICTIONAL characters can claim to have been in continuous publication, with new adventures featuring in as many as six magazines per month, for more than 65 years? Okay, there's that guy with the big "S" on his chest. But this book's not about him. It's about Batman. The Dark Knight Detective. The Guardian of Gotham.

The guy's a major household name. Even his supporting cast is familiar to the entire world: Robin, Batgirl, Commissioner Gordon, Alfred, the Joker, Catwoman. Well, I could go on and on. But that's what this book is for — to chronicle the long history of, in my professional opinion, the greatest comic book character ever devised.

Created by a teenaged Bob Kane in the 1930s, Batman combined the best of a dozen great fictional heroes (and a few villains). He's equal parts Sherlock Holmes, Zorro, Scarlet Pimpernel, Shadow, and Dracula; with a host of gadgets and vehicles that even James Bond could never equal. Batman's origin was the stuff of classic literature. An orphan alone in a cruel world that Dickens never dreamed up. The most self-made of all self-made men in popular culture. This guy can't fly or see through walls. He's not superfast and has no retractable claws or magic ring. He's just the guy that any of us could be if we dedicated our lives to being really smart, really athletic, and really scary. He's survived countless traps. He's been frozen, beaten, burnt, broken, and riddled with bullets. He even survived that silly TV series in the 1960s.

In fact, each decade seems to bring us a new Batman; never changing but adapted for the times. He was born of the Great Depression and his early tales are dark and brooding. In the 1940s he became more upbeat, more patriotic with an emphasis on detective work with his new sidekick, Robin the Boy Wonder. The 1950s saw him traveling to outer space or dealing with strange scientific anomalies created by the Atomic Age. In the tragically hip 1960s his adventures bordered on parody. The 1970s saw a return to his darker side with a more hardboiled approach to crime. In the 1980s we saw his darkest transformation into a haunted loner obsessed with the vow to his long dead parents. The 1990s saw more emphasis on stories on a grander, apocalyptic scale.

Through all of this Batman and company remained essentially the same. That just goes to show what an indestructible template this world of Gotham is.

And here, in your hands, is the world of Batman in the 21st century. This is the most exhaustive volume of Gotham lore ever compiled. Scott Beatty and the wizards at Dorling Kindersley have put together an invaluable reference that I know will have a permanent place by my keyboard. Bat-Gadgets and locales are shown in minute detail. The science and technology behind each is explained. Many of these images appear here for the first time. And the Rogues Gallery! All the most memorable foul fiends, twisted geniuses and career criminals that Batman has defeated or fought to a draw are given full biographical treatment. Batman's friends and allies are also here with their full histories and vital stats.

I wish I'd had this book ten years ago when I was first hired to write Batman adventures. It would have saved a lot of hours poring over old comic books. (But that was fun too!) The Batman universe is a fascinating one to play in and I love losing myself in it. As I say when I'm heading to the office to write, "Well, time to get back to Gotham City...."

Chuck Dixon
Fall, 2001

BATMAN'S WORLD

BRUCE WAYNE NEVER ASKED to be Batman. But no child wishes to be an orphan, especially young Bruce, whose parents were cruelly snatched away by a gunman's hand in a world that festers and feeds upon its own dark soul. Violence created the Dark Knight, and provided him with both the mission and the means by which Gotham City might be made a better place. In Bruce Wayne's mind the course is predetermined: he will bring law to the lawlessness of Gotham… or die trying. He is at war and the enemy is crime itself. His resolve indefatigable, his weapons inexhaustible, Batman has sacrificed every personal need – love, happiness, and his own peace of mind – in order to take back the Gotham night. Failure is not an option, nor is acquiescence. While enemies grow and casualties mount, the Dark Knight's resolve is only strengthened. He will fight on, however long it takes, to ensure that no other child is forced to witness the death of innocence.

Birth of the Batman

BRUCE WAYNE'S CHILDHOOD ended the night his parents were brutally murdered before his eyes in Gotham City's notorious Crime Alley. The young orphan swore a solemn oath to avenge their deaths, embarking on a worldwide odyssey to forge his mind and body into a living weapon. Years later, he returned to Gotham a master of virtually every known fighting discipline, as well as a cunning detective and relentless manhunter. Believing criminals to be "a cowardly and superstitious lot," Bruce crafted a new face to strike terror into their hearts. He would become a creature of the night, descending upon evil clothed in the mantle of the bat!

RANDOM VIOLENCE

The time was 10:47 p.m., a moment burned indelibly in Bruce Wayne's memory. As the Waynes were returning home from the cinema, Dr. Thomas Wayne was shot dead by a gun-toting hoodlum. Martha Wayne's screams for help were silenced by further bullets, leaving young Bruce sobbing beside his parents' still bodies on the trash-strewn pavement of Crime Alley as the unidentified gunman fled into the Gotham night.

A KIND STRANGER
After the questions of police and reporters, a grief-stricken Bruce was comforted by Dr. Leslie Thompkins. Her soothing words gave him the strength to quietly mourn his parents and to dedicate his life to honoring their memory in the pursuit of justice.

BELOW THE SURFACE

Though he swore to avenge his parents' deaths by warring on all criminals, young Bruce was unaware that a crucial part of his destiny lay quite literally right beneath his feet. As a toddler, he had fallen into the bat-infested limestone caves beneath Wayne Manor. And as an orphan child, those same bats haunted his nightmares with the rush of leathery wings. Only in adulthood would Bruce embrace the bat as inspiration.

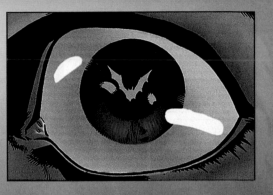

Whether Bruce realized it or not, the image of a bat was deeply-rooted in his childhood psyche.

WALKABOUT

At age 14, Bruce Wayne began his global sojourn, attending courses at Cambridge, the Sorbonne, and other European universities. Beyond academia, Bruce acquired more "practical" skills. Frenchman Henri Ducard made him an apprentice in manhunting. The ninja Kirigi schooled Bruce in stealth and the ways of the shadow warrior. African Bushmen taught hunting techniques, while Nepalese monks revealed healing arts. And so it went for 12 years as Bruce matured into manhood.

A LASTING IMPACT

There are 127 major styles of combat. While abroad, Bruce learned them all, from Aikido to Yaw-Yan. His knowledge of so many varied disciplines has made Bruce an unconventional and unpredictable opponent, quite capable of countering a Savate kick with a Capoeira dodge, then kayoing with a paw-knuckle strike!

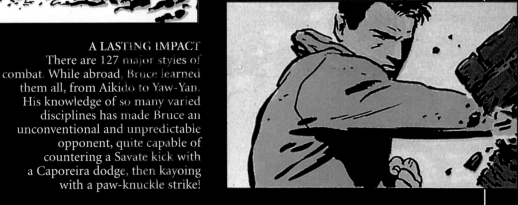

Batman's Look

THE FIRST NIGHT out was a disaster. Disguised as a street tough, Bruce Wayne's initial foray into vigilantism almost ended his life. Fear was the key, and a bat was the omen, crashing in fluttering frenzy through his study as he sat bleeding from his wounds. To strike terror, he would become as the bat, sketching out a symbolic costume which would have him clad from head to toe in stealthy black and gray against the Gotham night. With a scalloped cape fanning out into a winged silhouette, Batman would wear a grim cowl to mask identity and emotion, his mark emblazoned across his chest as an icon opposed to injustice!

DARK REFLECTIONS
Amid the gargoyles and parapets overlooking crime-ridden streets, Batman's own deliberately intimidating image blends seamlessly into the Gothic architecture pervading Gotham City.

CLOTHES MAKE THE MAN

He called it "a reconnaissance mission," stepping out among Gotham's dregs to see firsthand the hell to which his city had descended. Fully intending to avoid combat until he was truly ready, a disguised Bruce found trouble nonetheless, barely beating off his attackers before being shot and apprehended by the police. His years of training ensured his escape, but as he stumbled home to Wayne Manor, Bruce's patience was at an end. He could wait no longer, yet how could he win a war without first making his enemy fear him? Bruce waited for a sign.

CREATURES OF THE NIGHT
Whether by divine intervention or its own misguided sonar, a bat provided Bruce with the answer he needed. The very creature that had frightened him as a boy would share the secrets of instilling dread in the hearts of men.

PRIMAL FEAR
Believing criminals to be particularly cowardly and superstitious, Bruce designed the mantle of Batman to have a frightful impact, his dark mask and unfolding leathery cape paralyzing foes with utter terror!

BATMAN

REAL NAME: Bruce Wayne

OCCUPATION:
Industrialist/Philanthropist/
Crime Fighter

BASE: Gotham City

HEIGHT: 6 ft 2 in **WEIGHT:** 210 lb

EYES: Blue **HAIR:** Black

FIRST APPEARANCE:
DETECTIVE COMICS
#27 (May, 1939)

The Bat-Suit

POUND FOR POUND, body armor pales in comparison. Designed for maximum utility, the Dark Knight's costume is both fire-retardant and chemical-resistant, with triple-weave Kevlar positioned primarily around the torso's Bat-Symbol, an intentional and well-protected target. In addition, Batman's scalloped cape doubles as an offensive weapon: its weighted ends provide a physical wallop in tandem with its proven psychological impact upon criminals. The cowl – Kevlar-lined with a steel gorget – features various micro-electronics links, as well as night-vision technology to allow the Dark Knight to see in the dark. The main purpose of the Bat-Suit is to act as camouflage and to instill fear. Its basic design has remained virtually unchanged; however, it has been frequently updated to advance the Dark Knight's war on crime.

SPIRIT OF THE BAT
Even before a bat crashed into his study, Bruce Wayne had sensed the animal's iconic value. Spared a freezing death by a Native Alaskan shaman, Bruce learned of the bat's healing powers in Inuit folklore, a constant reminder in this ritual mask, the shaman's gift to him.

Directional microphone

Telescoping high-gain antenna

Hollow bat-ear assembly

Fiber-optic coaxial cable

Audio processor

THE TRANSFORMING MASK

Donning his cowl is a symbolic act for Batman. By putting it on, he reaffirms his oath to avenge the murders of his parents. Physically, the cowl allows the Dark Knight to mimic a bat's natural abilities with technology: Starlite lenses to stalk in utter darkness; aural-electronics to discern his prey's faintest whispers; and inertial navigators to keep him flying straight and true.

Field-of-view display projector

Starlite night-vision lens

Inertial navigation unit

Noise reduction speaker

THE COWL
Impacts to Batman's cowl are dissipated by a complex weave of selectable para-aramid fibers and exotic metal threads. The cowl's internal comm-link enables voice-command control of various equipment.

USING HIS HEAD
Optional Kevlar panels in the cowl provide extra protection over vulnerable skull areas – and also make Batman's head a useful weapon in close-quarters combat!

EMPOWERED
Bruce Wayne dons the Dark Knight's armor, his cape, and cowl, completing Batman's disguise.

Throat trauma protection

BEHIND THE MASK
The standard cowl (sans electronics) is sewn in a single-piece memory-weave pattern, stretching over Bruce's head and returning to normal shape. When not worn, the cowl folds into a wallet-sized unit. The entire costume is similarly compact.

Lightweight single-piece cowl

Integral ascender rail in glove for jumpline descent

Utility Belt

Nomex-reinforced fabric (15 micro-layers)

ALL WIRED UP
A "last resort" taser system is sewn into the outer layer of the Bat-suit atop an insulated internal lining. This one-shot defensive mechanism shocks up to 200,000 volts through a micro-thin electrode network dispersal over the entirety of Batman's costume. The taser is armed and fired via circuit-wafer controls in his gloves.

Tips of scalloped cape lead-weighted for offensive purposes

TAKING NO CHANCES
Electronic cooling systems in the breathable flame-retardant Nomex textile of the Bat-Suit provide comfortable wear even in raging conflagrations. The Kevlar-weave in Batman's cape and cowl offers high chemical-resistance and low electrical conductivity to external electrocution threats.

Climbing boots

BOOT DESIGN
Batman's steel-toed leather boots are augmented with Nomex-reinforced thermally-stable rubberized soles. Split asym slingshot heels flex with his ankles for full range of motion during building ascents.

THE UTILITY BELT

BATARANGS, monofilament cord jumplines, and gas bombs are just a few of the "equalizers" the Dark Knight conceals in his Utility Belt, perhaps the most sophisticated crime-fighting arsenal ever devised. Stowed in various compartments are the miniaturized tools and non-lethal deterrents Batman calls upon in his nocturnal vigil. With gas pellets, wireless transmitters, lock-picks, antitoxins, rebreathers and other sophisticated equipment, the belt is also armed with its own self-destruct mechanism to prevent nefarious tampering.

"Mother" electronics circuit board inside belt housing

Detachable palm-top communicator

Crime-scene recorder

Rebreather

Firing toggle

Collapsible grappling hook stowed behind buckle

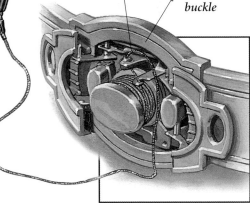

Removable buckle

Batarang compartment

MAXIMUM UTILITY
Batman's original Utility Belt, depicted here, was lightweight and streamlined. Its buckle concealed a spare jumpline and a CO_2-propelled grappling-hook launcher. During the No Man's Land period (see page 24), Batman adopted a bulkier version to carry additional weapons and supplies necessary for survival in quake-ruined Gotham City.

PENLIGHT
A precursor to his more-miniaturized fingerlight, Batman's earlier penlight provided ample nocturnal illumination. It was fitted with a rubberized mouth-grip to permit hands-free usage.

Infrared flash

Lens aperture

DIGITAL MICRO CAMERA

Lightweight titanium casing

Removable memory stick inside cylinder

Tear-gas pellet chambered for release

GAS PELLETS
Spring-loaded magazine cylinders in the belt are armed with various gas and chemical "pellets" of standard size. These include blinding smoke bombs, as well as disabling regurgitants and tear gases.

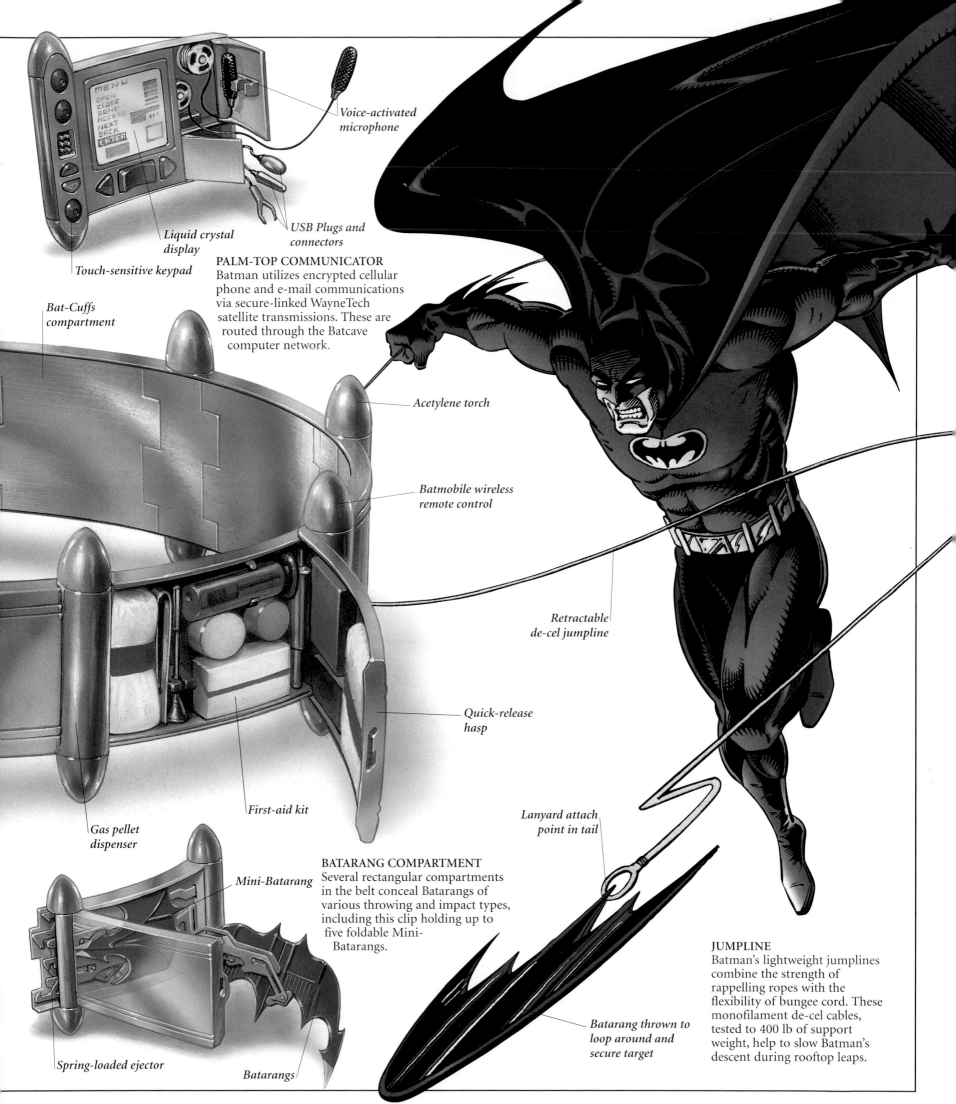

Voice-activated
microphone

USB Plugs and
connectors

Liquid crystal
display

Touch-sensitive keypad

PALM-TOP COMMUNICATOR
Batman utilizes encrypted cellular
phone and e-mail communications
via secure-linked WayneTech
satellite transmissions. These are
routed through the Batcave
computer network.

Bat-Cuffs
compartment

Acetylene torch

Batmobile wireless
remote control

Retractable
de-cel jumpline

Quick-release
hasp

First-aid kit

Lanyard attach
point in tail

Gas pellet
dispenser

Mini-Batarang

BATARANG COMPARTMENT
Several rectangular compartments
in the belt conceal Batarangs of
various throwing and impact types,
including this clip holding up to
five foldable Mini-
Batarangs.

JUMPLINE
Batman's lightweight jumplines
combine the strength of
rappelling ropes with the
flexibility of bungee cord. These
monofilament de-cel cables,
tested to 400 lb of support
weight, help to slow Batman's
descent during rooftop leaps.

Spring-loaded ejector

Batarangs

Batarang thrown to
loop around and
secure target

17

Bat-Weapons

BAT-CUFFS
These restraints are made of lightweight, sapphire-impregnated nylon overlaying a stranded-metal cable core. Only a diamond-edged cutting implement can sever these wrist-bands.

H E WOULDN'T USE A GUN – EVER. So indelible was the memory of his parents' fatal shootings that Bruce Wayne vowed never to take up firearms to fulfill his crime-fighting agenda. Justice, not vengeance, was his goal, requiring the Dark Knight to equip himself with non-lethal weapons. To make the Batman a real and visceral presence, penetrating grapnels would give the illusion of swooping flight high above Gotham's streets. Batarangs would meld razor-sharp *shuriken* with the Outback boomerang to create an unerring signature weapon. A potent array of chemical gas grenades and explosive capsules would provide just the right distractions needed to end a fight, while flexible, reinforced Bat-Cuffs would truss up his foes for the G.C.P.D. to haul away!

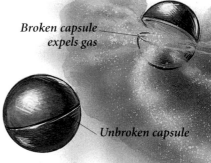

Rapid room-filling fogger

Floor-standing base

AEROSOL SPRAYS
Batman's miniaturized chemical arsenal includes IR paint markers, foaming explosive gels, super-cooled electronic device freezers, and Ver-Sed (quick-acting knock-out and temporary amnesiac) sprays.

Broken capsule expels gas

Unbroken capsule

GAS PELLETS
Various gas deterrents are arrayed in pouches throughout Batman's Utility Belt. Flash/Bang charges, smoke bombs, tear and regurgitant gases are deployed by breaking hardened-gelatin spheroid capsules.

BLOW-GUN
Bruce Wayne learned the subtle stealth of the blow-gun from Yanomami hunters along the mighty Amazon River. The Yanomami poisoned their prey; Batman prefers to tip his darts with fast-acting anesthetics.

WALL-PENETRATING GRAPNEL

Though not normally an offensive weapon, the Dark Knight's wall-penetrating grapnel is still an indispensable addition to his arsenal. A magazine of explosively-propelled darts attach to de-cel jumpline reels secured with braking and clipping mechanisms inside the grapnel gun sleeve. The grapnel allows Batman to scale up or rappel down tall buildings, or swing between Gotham skyscrapers on successive lines.

Micro-diamond drill head

PENETRATING DART
"Smart" acceleration motors within the grapnel dart head enable attachment to light aluminum, steel, or concrete masonry. The dart is also engineered for snap-on mini-carabiner or high-test de-cel line.

Firing button

Dart piercing concrete masonry

Dart magazine

Handle assembly with lanyard attach point

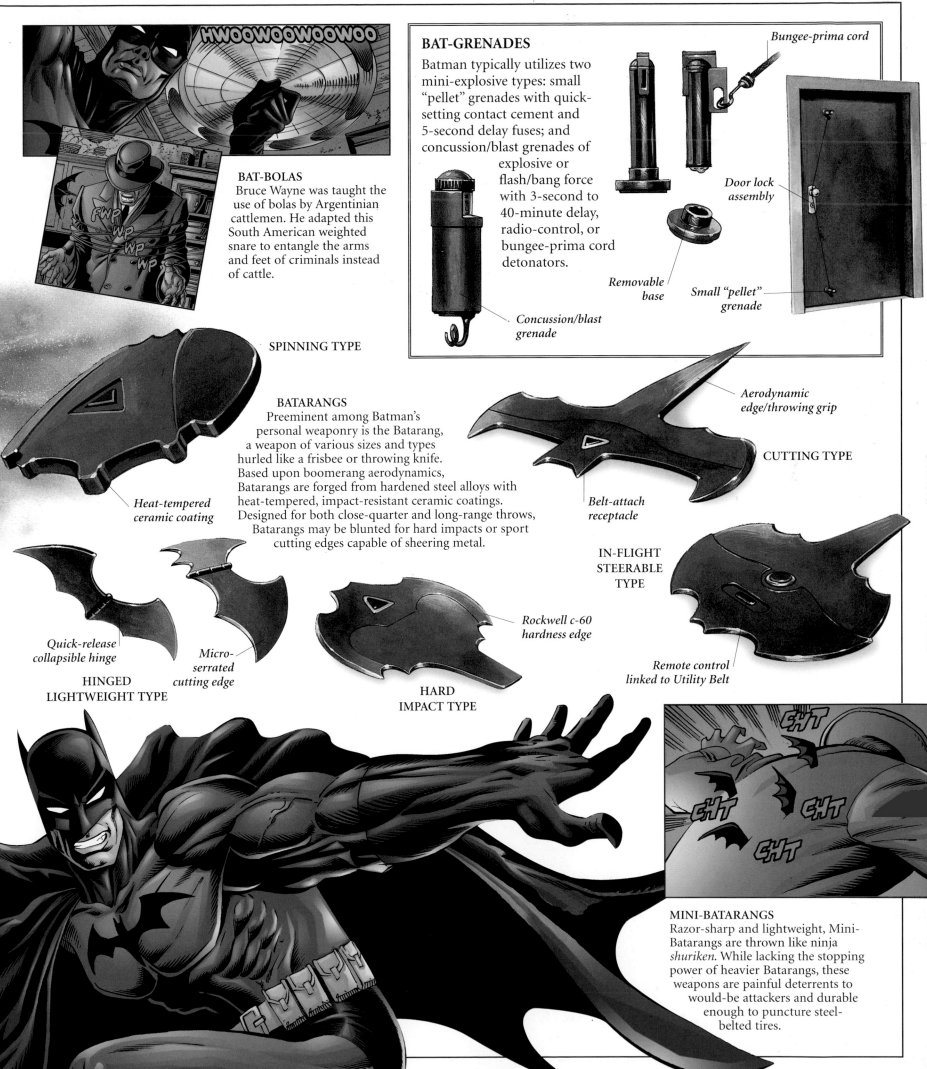

HWOOWOOWOOWOO

BAT-BOLAS
Bruce Wayne was taught the use of bolas by Argentinian cattlemen. He adapted this South American weighted snare to entangle the arms and feet of criminals instead of cattle.

BAT-GRENADES
Batman typically utilizes two mini-explosive types: small "pellet" grenades with quick-setting contact cement and 5-second delay fuses; and concussion/blast grenades of explosive or flash/bang force with 3-second to 40-minute delay, radio-control, or bungee-prima cord detonators.

Bungee-prima cord

Door lock assembly

Removable base

Small "pellet" grenade

Concussion/blast grenade

SPINNING TYPE

BATARANGS
Preeminent among Batman's personal weaponry is the Batarang, a weapon of various sizes and types hurled like a frisbee or throwing knife. Based upon boomerang aerodynamics, Batarangs are forged from hardened steel alloys with heat-tempered, impact-resistant ceramic coatings. Designed for both close-quarter and long-range throws, Batarangs may be blunted for hard impacts or sport cutting edges capable of sheering metal.

Aerodynamic edge/throwing grip

CUTTING TYPE

Heat-tempered ceramic coating

Belt-attach receptacle

IN-FLIGHT STEERABLE TYPE

Quick-release collapsible hinge

HINGED LIGHTWEIGHT TYPE

Micro-serrated cutting edge

Rockwell c-60 hardness edge

HARD IMPACT TYPE

Remote control linked to Utility Belt

CHT

MINI-BATARANGS
Razor-sharp and lightweight, Mini-Batarangs are thrown like ninja *shuriken*. While lacking the stopping power of heavier Batarangs, these weapons are painful deterrents to would-be attackers and durable enough to puncture steel-belted tires.

19

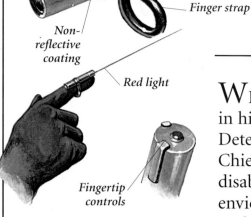

Impact-resistant casing

Finger strap

Non-reflective coating

Red light

Fingertip controls

BAT-GADGETS

Rotating selector sleeve

Hardened tool steel case

FINGERLIGHT
Powered by a rechargeable micro fuel cell, the Fingerlight can be worn on any digit. White, red, and infrared radial LEDs provide focused or wide-angle collimated 10,000 micro-candela beams via touch-sensitive fingertip controls.

WITH A HOST OF MINIATURIZED TOOLS concealed in his Utility Belt and Batmobile, the Dark Knight Detective takes a hi-tech approach to sleuthing. Chief among his investigative arsenal is his electronics-disabling Universal Tool. Most forensics labs would be envious of Batman's Crime Scene Kit, complete with mobile micro gas chromatograph. Even more ambitious are his satellite-linked Mini-Computer and Batmobile-propelling Remote System Controller. And no less useful to Batman's crime-busting are his fingerlight, gas masks, multifunction binoculars, tracers, and other invaluable scientific devices.

TOOLS OF THE TRADE

During his decade-long quest to hone his body to physical perfection, Bruce Wayne immersed himself in the study of electronics, computers, and all the hi-tech trappings of an increasingly scientific-savvy criminal element. As quantum leaps were made in forensics and evidence detection, Bruce made certain that the tools of his crime-fighting crusade reflected the most advanced technology available. And if WayneTech research could not provide a required piece of equipment, Bruce would acquire the skills to make it himself!

Unfolding sequence

Interchangeable tool points

TOOL KIT
A rotating selector sleeve places drive unit over required tool. The kit includes wire-cutters and strippers, electro-lockpicking device, as well as torx, box, and star drive tool points.

Fully deployed

MINI-COMPUTER
Fully-collapsible, with an 86% standard keyboard and rechargeable fuel cells, the computer features 2.6 gigahertz CPU, DOS and non-DOS BIOS compact chip-sets, secure-signal cellular phone, digital fax/modem, GPS, and CD-ROM player/burner. A Remote System Controller is detachable from the unit.

Pre-labeled sample bags

High-resolution flat-screen display

Free-standing multi-spectral camera

Batmobile Remote System Controller

Sample analyzer

CRIME SCENE KIT
This contains a multi-spectral high-resolution camera with still-shot and video functions, micro gas chromatograph, sample bags and blood-drying bags in various sizes, fingerprinting materials (traditional dusts, cyanoacrylate adhesive used to lift fingerprints), and direct-link software to forensics hardware in the Bat-Suit, Batcave, and Batmobile.

Storage for tool points

MULTIFUNCTION BINOCULARS
A high-resolution digital interface allows viewing with conventional, infrared, and ultraviolet imaging. Other features include light-amplification and "bloom suppression" to reduce glare. Holographic lensing and digital-zoom combine for 60X further magnification in addition to still-frame photographic capture.

EPROM reader/writer

Positive-grip collar on selector sleeve

RS-232 logic-controlled breakout box

USB jack

CPU breakout box

TRACER DEVICE
A micro GPS tracer in Batman's boot heel allows Alfred and allies to track his whereabouts. To watch criminals, Batman employs limited-range 27 mm-wide "burr" tracers, as well as 22 mm-diameter rubber-edged "throwing" tracers with digital pulse radio links to Utility Belt relays.

Electronic probes

Oscilloscope/vector scope display

Multi-line analyzer

Broadband/HDTV jack

GAS MASK
In addition to compact conventional gas masks stored in six-pack Utility Belt magazines, Batman carries a more durable gas mask with positive-seal integral mouthpiece. This mask is designed for "full-spectrum" deployment, able to protect against a wide variety of nuclear, biological, and chemical agents.

UNIVERSAL TOOL
No more than 9 in long and weighing a mere 3.2 lb, Batman's electronics "catch-all" is powered by rechargeable mini fuel cells and includes a full lineman's suite of miniaturized equipment in a single hardened tool-steel case. This doubles as a convenient hammer.

Tap

Jumper

Foldable filter cartridge

Pull-open facial skin protection layer

21

Gotham City

Gotham City is one of the oldest-established Eastern urban centers in the US. It nestles at the mouth of the turbid Gotham River upon islands once peopled by the vanished Miagani tribe of Native Americans. Though it now resides in infamy for its rampant *per capita* crime rate, florid urban legends, and brooding Gothic spires, Gotham's 19th-century patrons once envisioned their community as a concrete and steel stronghold for pious righteousness and booming industrial growth. Bolstered for generations by the business ventures of the wealthy Wayne family, Gotham's economy has indeed helped the city to flourish as a technological hub, but one founded upon the swampy soils of slow and inexorable moral decay, despite the best of intentions.

URBAN LEGEND
Since few Gothamites have witnessed his exploits, the Batman is believed by many to be an urban myth created to frighten naughty children or deter the criminals prowling Gotham City's dark streets.

SANCTUARY

Historians possess no concise annals detailing the 17th-century origins of Gotham Village, which remain a mystery. However, the chilling "Penitence Tale of Gotham" establishes that the hamlet's very first dwelling was, in fact, an asylum predating the city's infamous Arkham madhouse. As the story goes, a devoutly religious mulatto named Hiram (surname, if any, unknown) abandoned plans to erect a chapel of faith when London-born Epsilpah Clevenger implicated himself and Hiram in a web of murder. By Clevenger's insistence, Hiram's church became a sanatorium, and if the legend is to be believed, Gotham's first two residents were self-confessed killers!

FORTRESS GOTHAM
The bleak Gothic ramparts designed by architect Cyrus Pinkney were intended by Judge Solomon Wayne to be a bulwark against iniquity. But Pinkney's numerous critics argue that his controversial constructions effectively barricaded vice within the city.

CIVIC DUTY

Batman is by no means the only heroic presence associated with the city that once boasted the headquarters of the mighty Justice Society of America. Gotham has also been home to the original Green Lantern and to the Black Canary. Other masked vigilantes waging private war on wrongdoing have included the Ragman, Black Lightning, Joe Public, Geist, Pagan, and teenager Lonnie Machin, who attempted to abolish Gotham's "inadequate system of justice" as the authority-bashing Anarky (right).

MEAN STREETS

Bruce Wayne once described Gotham as an anvil upon which "one is broken or tempered," an apt comparison given his own tragic boyhood experience in the notorious Crime Alley.

No Man's Land

COLLATERAL DAMAGE
After the quake, Batman and Robin watched helplessly as city workers struggled to dispose of the dead and stave off the threat of plague from rats and rotting corpses. Soon, mass funeral pyres joined the raging fires further crippling Gotham.

VOICE IN THE DARK
Talk radio host Vesper Fairchild continued to broadcast after the quake, in a vain attempt to bring hope to the survivors of Gotham.

GOTHAM FACED ITS DARKEST HOURS. Having just barely contained "The Clench," a virulent outbreak of Ebola Gulf-A which killed thousands, Gotham City was ill-prepared when the Cataclysm struck. The earthquake's tremors measured a staggering 7.6 on the Richter Scale, but its aftershocks were far more unsettling. Declared a Federal "No Man's Land" by the US Government, Gotham's bridges were dynamited and its arteries to the civilized world were severed. But the Dark Knight would not concede. Even as Gotham devolved into violent fiefdoms lorded over by liberated criminals and industrious street gangs, Batman and his closest associates remained, fighting from within to take the city back one sector at a time.

BLACK MONDAY

Day One of NML would be known in infamy as "Black Monday." Those unfortunates left behind endured feudal rule by the likes of the Joker, Two-Face, and other freed Arkham villains, as well as persecution from the Demonz, LoBoys, and Xhosa gangs. But even as Gotham was carved asunder, the Blue Boys – James Gordon's vigilante squad of loyal cops – struggled to maintain order in the face of marauders on every side.

"NO ONE HAD THE POWER TO *STOP* THEM.

"NO ONE COULD TURN ASIDE THE TRAGEDY.

"BUT THAT'S NOT THE CASE *TODAY*."

FALLING DOWN

Before the No Man's Land edict, an exodus of Gotham refugees resulted in tragedy when fleeing citizens jammed the Vincefinkel Bridge. The weakened span collapsed under their weight, sending thousands to watery graves at the bottom of the miry Gotham River.

WAYNE IN WASHINGTON

Bruce Wayne was Gotham City's last hope. Believing dark forces to be behind the push for the city's dissolution, he accompanied Mayor Marion Grange to Capitol Hill and lobbied for Gotham's stay of execution. Mayor Grange fell victim to an assassin's bullet meant for Wayne himself, whose impassioned speech before Congress failed to avert the disaster of No Man's Land.

FEUDAL RULES

As Gotham was torn apart by rival factions, Oracle began her record of life in NML. She mapped the liberated territories "tagged" by the Dark Knight in spray-paint as he fought to reclaim the city.

SCRATCH

From rock star to political mover and shaker: charismatic Nicholas Scratch positioned himself to be the architect of Gotham's disintegration. He gathered public support for Gotham's "death warrant" so that he might take control of the city.

GOTHAM REBUILT

LEX LUTHOR SUCCEEDED where Bruce Wayne failed. Openly defying Congressional edict, the power-hungry Metropolis mogul capitalized on public opinion rallying to reverse Gotham City's status as a condemned No Man's Land. While the US Government argued whether or not Gotham deserved a second chance at life, Luthor set his plans in motion, descending upon Gotham and establishing his "Camp Lex" in Grant Park as a beachhead for re-taking the city. After fierce debate, Congress reneged and the ambitious "Billion Dollar Build-Up" Federal Works Project began, teaming LexCorp, STAR Labs, Wayne Enterprises and its charitable arm the Wayne Foundation, as well as the US Army Corps of Engineers in rebuilding Gotham from the ground up.

MASTER BUILDER
Lex Luthor's plans to rebuild Gotham were wholly motivated by corporate greed. Even while galvanizing Gotham's residents to pull together and dig their way out of NML, he plotted to destroy the city's property records so that he could seize any land he desired.

GOTHIC TO GLASS
New Gotham's skyline is an amalgam of yesterdays and tomorrows. Newly-erected towers of glass stand side-by-side with granite Gothic citadels preserved from the old city. This dichotomy of architecture appeals to both native Gothamites and the city's teeming newcomers, the latter attracted to the blank slate afforded by a reborn Gotham. The city once described as a "sinkhole of corruption" now looks forward to a hard-won era of peace and prosperity.

Luthor's Amazonian bodyguard Mercy

ARCHITECT OF HOPE
By committing the construction might of his company LexCorp to rebuilding Gotham City, Lex Luthor scored an incomparable public relations coup. But while Luthor's efforts were lauded as worthy of a Nobel Prize, the power-hungry tycoon had his eyes on a more lucrative trophy. As LexCorp re-rooted itself in Gotham's financial district, Luthor capitalized on his new humane image to make a successful bid for the US Presidency!

MASS TRANSIT

While repairs to Gotham's antiquated subway continue, commuters can now travel on the new Rapid Transit System monorail. Spiraling through Gotham on 134 miles of elevated track, the G.R.T.S. monorail is the world's longest independently-operated conveyance.

LexCom

THE REBUILDING OF GOTHAM

1 WAYNE MANOR
2 BRENTWOOD ACADEMY
3 CRIME ALLEY
4 ARKHAM ASYLUM
5 ROBINSON PARK
6 WAYNE TOWER
7 ORACLE'S CLOCKTOWER
8 G.C.P.D. HEADQUARTERS
9 CATHEDRAL SQUARE
10 BLACKGATE ISLE

GOTHAM CITY

LAVISH LIFE
To the Gotham public, Bruce Wayne seems only concerned with fast cars, faster women, and all the luxuries of a jet-setting mogul.

BRUCE WAYNE

BRUCE WAYNE DOES NOT EXIST. In many ways, Bruce Wayne also perished the night his parents were murdered in Crime Alley all those years ago. In Bruce's own mind, Batman became the dominant reality from that moment forward as his quest for justice overshadowed all other personal needs or desires. So single-minded in his crusade, Bruce thinks of himself only as the Dark Knight. The bored billionaire playboy Bruce Wayne – so well known to Gotham City – is merely a ruse, distracting all those around him from the fact that his beneficent concerns take a decidedly more hands-on approach when day turns to night and the Batman changes into his "working clothes."

MOST ELIGIBLE BACHELOR

For a bevy of starlets, sirens, and socialites, Bruce Wayne will always be "the one that got away." Though spied by paparazzi on the arms of such fetching beauties as diva LaDonna Diaz or cover-girl Lydia Granger, the confirmed bachelor, so often "called away on business," rarely finishes a late-night tryst. This only makes Bruce's potential paramours all the more ardent, each convinced she might be the one to finally reel him in.

DOG DAZE
While purchasing hot dogs for a hungry date, Bruce – unable to reveal Batman's combat skills – prevented a robbery by temporarily blinding the would-be thief with a squirt of mustard!

A CLEAR HEAD
Beneath the façade of the hard-living billionaire bachelor, Bruce Wayne is a devout teetotaler.

LOST IN THE PART

By imparting his own theatrical expertise, Alfred Pennyworth has helped Bruce to maintain his dashing playboy persona. But when Bruce seemed "lost in the part" after meeting the bedazzling Poison Ivy, Alfred cooled his employer's ardor and brought him back to reality with a cold shower.

CLICK

ON THE COUCH

Occasionally, the worlds of Bruce Wayne and Batman collide. When Bruce submitted to a psychological profile to maintain his WayneCorp insurance benefits, he unsuspectingly played into the hands of a foe who knew his secret identity. As the nefarious Professor Hugo Strange manipulated Bruce's mind, the masks of billionaire and Batman began to slip!

IDENTITY CRISIS

But even as Strange gloated, Bruce had a plan. To make the evil doctor doubt the Dark Knight's secret, Bruce compelled himself to repress his own alter-ego, inducing partial amnesia to forget he ever was Batman. Meanwhile, Nightwing and Robin raced to defeat Strange!

Loved and Lost

VICKY VALE
Photo-journalist Vicki Vale's camera never lied, nor did her boyfriend Bruce Wayne. But he never told her about his alter-ego Batman either, despite many heart-wrenching attempts. As Vicki drew closer, Bruce retreated behind the veil of his secret identity, suffering in silence as he pushed her away forever.

SOMETIMES LOVE can be the greatest foe of all. Although the Dark Knight's relentless crusade ill affords time for dedication to affairs of the heart, Batman has found himself distracted by romance more than once. In the seemingly endless queue of beautiful women spied on the arm of billionaire Bruce Wayne, only a handful have glimpsed the "real" man behind the bored playboy façade. And of this chosen few, the names Julie, Vicki, Talia, Silver, Shondra, Kathy, Vesper, and Ivy have all given the Dark Knight significant pause over the years. In her own way, each of these women has forced Bruce to choose between true love and the war he has pledged to fight until his dying day.

THE HEART OF THE BAT

Batman protects his heart with body armor; Bruce Wayne shields his by being distant and aloof. Bruce has surrendered to the realization that true happiness will always be secondary to his crusade. He has accepted loneliness as his lot in life, convinced that he can accomplish a greater good by sacrificing companionship for devotion to his cause. Knowing the constant dangers he faces, Bruce is reluctant to make love another casualty of his war on crime.

DR. SHONDRA KINSOLVING
Before Bruce could reveal his feelings to personal physician Shondra Kinsolving, Bane crippled him. Shondra, meanwhile, was kidnapped by her evil half-brother Benedict Asp, who warped her latent empathic abilities to evil. Though Bruce defeated Asp and rescued Shondra, the damage to her mind was too great. As she healed Bruce's lingering injuries, Shondra's psyche regressed into childhood.

KATHY KANE
When Bruce dreamt of the future, he often found Kathy Kane – once the girl-gangbuster Batwoman – the focus of an idyllic life with the Dark Knight happily married and satisfyingly retired. But neither Bruce and Kathy, nor their masked alter-egos, ever acted upon their mutual attraction. And when the lovely circus owner was killed by the League of Assassins' Bronze Tiger, it was far too late.

TALIA
No other woman has kindled greater passion in Batman than the daughter of Rā's al Ghūl. But the Dark Knight will not compromise his devotion to justice for perhaps the love of his life.

SILVER ST. CLOUD

Bruce met convention organizer Silver St. Cloud during a charity benefit aboard his yacht. Even then Silver believed Bruce to be more than he appeared, a suspicion later confirmed when the Dark Knight crashed through Gotham's Expo Center in a struggle with an assassin. Silver recognized her suitor, confessing her love to Batman in a tearful farewell rather than bear seeing him risk his life night after night.

PAMELA ISLEY

When Poison Ivy robbed the Danzig Charity gala Bruce was attending, he knew that his attraction was more lust than love, and rooted in Ivy's spellbinding pheromones. Her first kiss is poison; the second its antidote. When they first met, Ivy's toxic lips planted a seed of toxic rapture in Bruce. But when she later kissed a dying Dark Knight, Ivy unknowingly cured her intended victim and established a budding sexual tension between them!

JULIE MADISON

Bruce's first love, aspiring actress Julie Madison, was completely convinced by her paramour's playboy pretense. But until Bruce was willing to "make something of himself," Julie knew their relationship faced its final curtain call. Ending her engagement to Bruce, Julie cast a new life for herself in Hollywood as starlet Portia Storme.

VESPER FAIRCHILD

Just as Bruce began to acknowledge his ardor for WKGC DJ and "Siren of the Night" Vesper Fairchild, the city's great earthquake fractured their relationship. Vesper chose to leave Bruce and Gotham behind during No Man's Land, a decision she regretted on her return to the rebuilt city. Only time will tell if their love will find more solid footing... or remain on shaky ground.

Wayne Enterprises

CONSIDERED THE BACKBONE of Gotham, Wayne Enterprises and its various subsidiary corporations employ the largest portion of the city's considerable work-force. From wealth amassed by the extensive real-estate holdings of Judge Solomon Wayne, His Honor's heirs established Wayne Shipping and Wayne Chemical, companies energized by America's booming Industrial Revolution. As the 20th century dawned, WayneCorp and its fledgling aviation division ushered the city past the woes of the Great Depression and two World Wars. Today, WayneTech and Wayne Aerospace stand at the forefront of pharmaceutical and technological research and development. The charitable Wayne Foundation reinvests the fruits of the Wayne holdings' labors in philanthropic endeavors at home and abroad.

THE WAYNE BUILDING
Erected in 1939, the Wayne Building – headquarters of WayneCorp and the Wayne Foundation – is one of the few remaining landmarks of Old Gotham to survive the city's great earthquake. At 78 stories (1, 207 ft to the tip of its antenna), the Wayne Building is also Gotham's tallest pre-quake structure. It continues to be the nerve center of the city's financial district.

AFTER THE CRASH

Wayne Enterprises is perhaps the only Gotham-based corporation to weather the city's calamitous earthquake and year of No Man's Land. The company ensured its continued survival by transferring the burden of its manufacturing to satellite facilities elsewhere. Profits earned during NML were some of the first capital funds applied to the city's eventual rebuilding. Without hesitation, Wayne Enterprises exceeded Lex Luthor's investments in Gotham's future.

LUCIUS FOX: THE MIDAS TOUCH

Lucius Fox is one of the most sought-after businessmen in the world, a president and CEO with the power to turn gold into platinum. Graduating *magna cum laude* from the Morton Business School, Fox maneuvered Atwater Air from near-bankruptcy to overnight success, with stock options soaring as high as the company's commuter jets. But Fox's greatest challenge has been his corporate restructuring of Wayne Enterprises, handling day-to-day business operations for Bruce Wayne, as well as nurturing Dick Grayson's impressive stock portfolio.

POWER NAP
To his employees, billionaire Bruce Wayne is just another member of the idle rich, whiling away the workday morning dreaming of an early afternoon tee-off at the Bristol Links Country Club's golf course.

IN THE BLACK
Fox wonders if WayneTech's research into integrated infrared and thermal-imaging equipment, so-called night-vision technology, is worth the estimated $2 million deficit of "mis-ground optics" listed on inter-office damage reports.

FINANCIAL LOSSES
Meticulous in balancing Wayne Enterprises' ledgers, Lucius Fox is mystified to discover "shrinkage inventory" valued at nine figures or more. Little does he know that this lost company property has been misappropriated by owner Bruce Wayne himself for the Dark Knight's personal use!

COMPANY CARS
Wayne Industries' automotive division produces some of the world's most advanced race engines, yet design specs for the division's latest models often seem to slip through digital cracks during inter-office e-mail transmission, while experimental units vanish from warehouse storage.

GENERATING INCOME
A missing WayneTech prototype hydrogen generator, a clean and efficient electrical source, produced its fuel via biophotolysis of the green algae *Chlaymydomonas MGA 161* and the bacterium *Rhodovulum sulfidophilum W-1S*. Now it powers the Batcave!

HOISTED ASSETS
Wayne Shipping is at a loss to explain a purloined 10-ton capacity rail crane. Leased from Gotham's Met-Rail, this invaluable piece of heavy equipment went missing from the company's Tricorner Yards division. Wayne Enterprises was forced to pay the crane's manufacturer more than $1.5 million as reimbursement.

SKYROCKETING DIVIDENDS
Even more curious is the case of a military contract C-130 transport plane, one of several aircraft including W4 Wraith fighters and Kestrel attack helicopters which have disappeared right off Wayne Aviation and Aerospace's radar, never to return. Furthermore, modifications to Bruce Wayne's SlipStream corporate jet far outweigh the cost of the plane itself!

COMMISSIONER GORDON

JIM GORDON BELIEVES in the Batman. A former Chicago police captain, Gordon's transfer to Gotham City paralleled the Dark Knight's emergence as costumed crime fighter. This coincidence has bound them inextricably since their first fateful meeting. Assigned to capture the urban legend stalking Gotham's lawbreakers, Gordon instead forged an uneasy alliance with the mysterious vigilante while rooting out the very real internal corruption plaguing the G.C.P.D.. In time, Gordon would be named Commissioner and the Dark Knight would become a trusted ally in policing Gotham's streets. This partnership, however, has exacted a heavy toll on Gordon's own health and the lives of his most cherished loved ones. A mutual sense of shared tragedy has bound him and Batman even closer together.

THE LONG GOODBYE

After more than 20 years on the force, three bullets convinced Jim Gordon it was time to retire. Still recovering from the near-fatal shooting which united the Gotham Police and the Bat-Family in hunting down his assailant, Gordon left the G.C.P.D. a better place, though a much lonelier one for the Dark Knight.

COMMISSIONER GORDON

REAL NAME: James W. Gordon
OCCUPATION:
Retired Police Commissioner
BASE: Gotham City
HEIGHT: 5 ft 9 in **WEIGHT:** 168 lb
EYES: Blue **HAIR:** White
FIRST APPEARANCE:
DETECTIVE COMICS #27
(May, 1939)

THE PRICE OF LOVE

Although Barbara Gordon loved her husband, she soon came to realize that Jim was even more married to his badge! Despite frequent disagreements, they stayed together for the sake of their two young children, son James Jr. and adopted daughter Barbara. In time, Jim and Barbara divorced amicably, with Jim retaining custody of their daughter.

Barbara Gordon left Gotham City for good, taking their son with her.

SARAH ESSEN-GORDON

Gordon met Det. Sgt. Sarah Essen when she was assigned to his "Batman Task Force" years ago. Mutual attraction led to a brief and passionate affair, which Essen broke off. Later, the two reunited and married. However, their happiness would be tragically short-lived.

LIFE FOR LIFE

When the Joker abducted the first 36 newborn children of NML Gotham in a plot to crush the fragile morale of the city, Sarah Gordon gave her life to save them. As she caught an infant callously thrown by the Ace of Knaves, she dropped her gun. While Sarah shielded the baby in her arms, the Joker mercilessly shot her.

MERRY CHRISTMAS

Ironically, the Joker found no humor in Sarah's death.

Gordon packs a mean left hook!

STREET TOUGH

Once a cop, always a cop. Gordon is licensed to carry his service pistol, a Browning BDAO 9-mm automatic. For extra protection, he conceals a Smith & Wesson .38 Police Special revolver in a "hold-out" ankle holster. But even without a gun, the streetwise Gordon knows how to start and finish a fight.

GOTHAM'S FINEST

BADGE OF HONOR
Marked by a critical personnel shortage after Gotham's millennial reopening, the G.C.P.D. initiated a recruitment drive to bolster its thinned ranks. The program targeted enterprising young men and women yearning to improve the quality of life in the city.

DET. RENEE MONTOYA
The daughter of Dominican immigrants, Renee Montoya has worked long and hard to earn her detective's shield. As a beat cop, she apprehended escaped serial killer Mr. Zsasz, proving her mettle to a predominately male police precinct.

THANKS TO NO MAN'S LAND, the Gotham City Police Department has earned a new level of public respect. Dubbed the "Blue Boys" during that terrible year, a cadre of Gotham cops led by Jim Gordon remained behind to keep the peace in the quake-devastated and isolated city. With Gotham rebuilt, Gordon has retired, knowing that a few honest cops remain, including new Commissioner Michael Akins and Chief of Police Mackenzie "Hardback" Bock. As before, Lt. Harvey Bullock's Major Crimes Unit boasts detectives Renee Montoya, Crispus Allen, Joely Bartlett, Vincent Del Arrazio, Dagmar Procjnow, Tommy Burke, Ivan Cohen, and Andrea "Andi" Kasinski among its officers.

BULLOCK'S LAW

Harvey Bullock has but three vices: donuts, a good cigar, and old movies. Admittedly rough around the edges, the former sergeant finds his role commanding the G.C.P.D. Major Crimes Unit an uncomfortable fit, even with Gotham battling the same old problems. Organized crime has re-established itself, with at least five cartels vying for supremacy. And in addition to the usual costumed villainy, Gotham faces civil turmoil with "OGs" (Original Gothamites) threatening "Deezees" – returned citizens who supposedly "deserted" the city during NML.

Officer Dan Foley

Det. Renee Montoya

DET. CRISPUS ALLEN
Though she thinks her partner arrogant and intractable, Montoya respects the intensity Crispus Allen – a former Metropolis homicide detective – brings to his new post in Gotham. When accused of "moral superiority," Allen chalks it up to his own unwavering belief in the law.

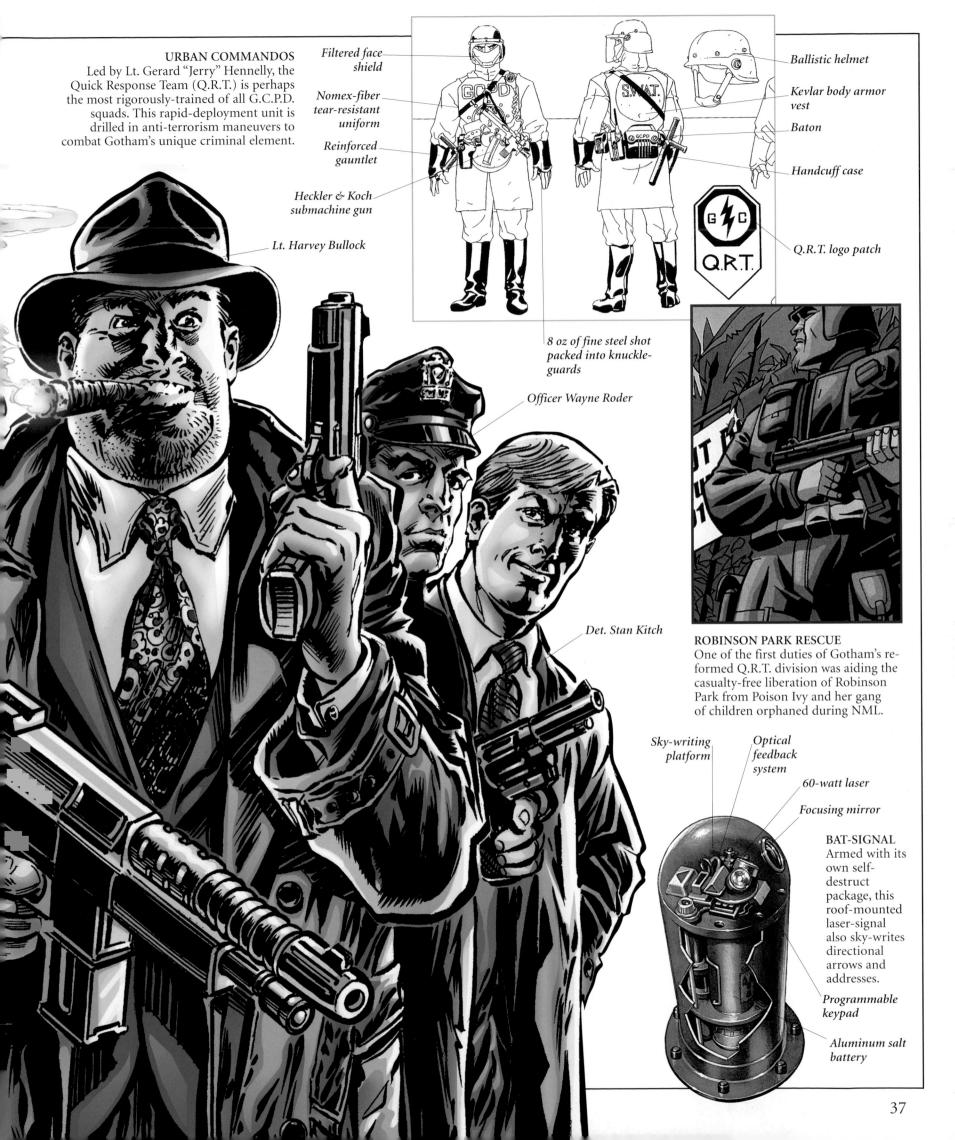

URBAN COMMANDOS
Led by Lt. Gerard "Jerry" Hennelly, the Quick Response Team (Q.R.T.) is perhaps the most rigorously-trained of all G.C.P.D. squads. This rapid-deployment unit is drilled in anti-terrorism maneuvers to combat Gotham's unique criminal element.

Filtered face shield

Nomex-fiber tear-resistant uniform

Reinforced gauntlet

Heckler & Koch submachine gun

Lt. Harvey Bullock

Ballistic helmet

Kevlar body armor vest

Baton

Handcuff case

Q.R.T. logo patch

8 oz of fine steel shot packed into knuckle-guards

Officer Wayne Roder

Det. Stan Kitch

ROBINSON PARK RESCUE
One of the first duties of Gotham's re-formed Q.R.T. division was aiding the casualty-free liberation of Robinson Park from Poison Ivy and her gang of children orphaned during NML.

Sky-writing platform

Optical feedback system

60-watt laser

Focusing mirror

BAT-SIGNAL
Armed with its own self-destruct package, this roof-mounted laser-signal also sky-writes directional arrows and addresses.

Programmable keypad

Aluminum salt battery

Wayne Manor

OLD WAYNE MANOR
Once a hub of charity balls and Gotham glitterati, the Wayne mansion grew cold and lonely after the deaths of Bruce's parents.

STATELY HOME to the Wayne family for nearly 150 years, Wayne Manor overlooks Gotham City from the wealthy Crest Hill community of Bristol Township. The sprawling mansion was commissioned by railroad mogul Jerome K. van Derm in 1855, but was unoccupied until Solomon Zebediah Wayne – Bruce Wayne's great-great-grandfather – and his brother Joshua set up residence in 1858. Domicile to the generations of Waynes who followed, the Manor sadly fell victim to Gotham's terrible earthquake. His home damaged beyond repair, Bruce Wayne reluctantly elected to totally redesign the Manor, erecting a veritable fortress inspired by the Gothic edifices of Old Gotham architect Cyrus Pinkney. High battlements and parapets adorn the modern Manor, making it a fitting sanctuary for the Dark Knight who dwells within.

Norman tower

Turret

Parapet

ANCESTRAL TIES
A castle befits Bruce Wayne's ancestry. While his great-grandmother belonged to the MacDubh clan of Scotland, a more distant relative was Sir Gaweyne de Weyne, a French knight of the Scottish Court who fought and died in the Crusades.

Stonework from original manor house

25-pound cannon (forged 1864)

HOME WRECKER
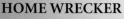
Though his properties in Gotham had been quake-proofed, Bruce Wayne's own home was not. Wayne Manor sat directly above a geological fault-line. When the tectonic plates slipped, the Manor was cleaved in half, collapsing into the Batcave below.

CASTLE OF THE BAT
The new Wayne Manor is a pastiche of Gothic architecture combined with the castle dwellings of Bruce's own Scottish and Norman roots. The Manor's foundations are composed of aggregate salvaged from the original mansion, while its formidable turrets – shipped to Gotham stone by stone – once belonged to the 15th-century Scottish keep of the MacDubh clan.

UNDERGROUND RAILROAD
During the Civil War, the brothers Wayne hid Southern slaves in the caverns beneath Wayne Manor, an artery of the "Underground Railroad" leading to freedom in the North. The cannon that guards the Manor was a gift to Solomon Wayne from a Harvard classmate and fellow opponent of slavery.

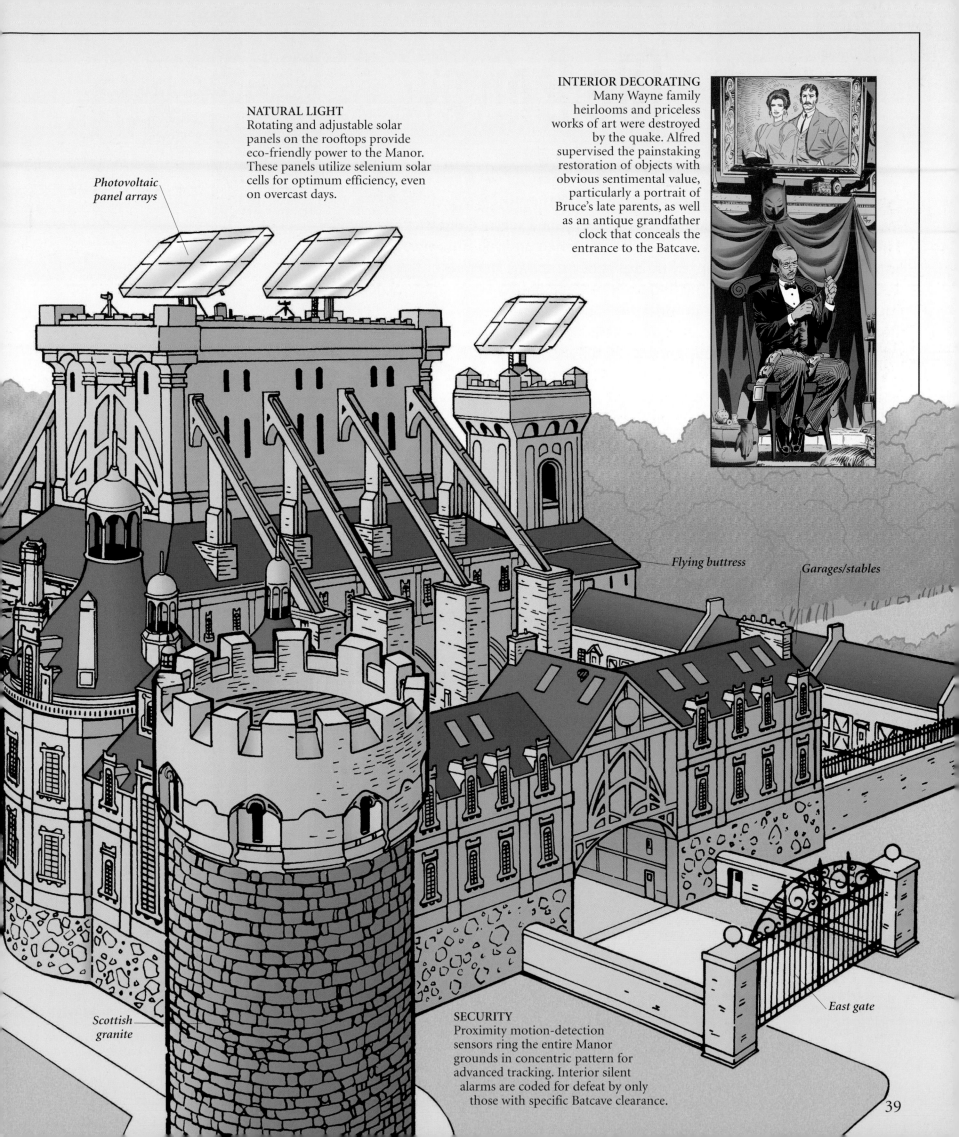

NATURAL LIGHT
Rotating and adjustable solar panels on the rooftops provide eco-friendly power to the Manor. These panels utilize selenium solar cells for optimum efficiency, even on overcast days.

Photovoltaic panel arrays

INTERIOR DECORATING
Many Wayne family heirlooms and priceless works of art were destroyed by the quake. Alfred supervised the painstaking restoration of objects with obvious sentimental value, particularly a portrait of Bruce's late parents, as well as an antique grandfather clock that conceals the entrance to the Batcave.

Flying buttress

Garages/stables

Scottish granite

SECURITY
Proximity motion-detection sensors ring the entire Manor grounds in concentric pattern for advanced tracking. Interior silent alarms are coded for defeat by only those with specific Batcave clearance.

East gate

THE BATCAVE

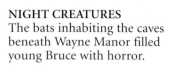

NIGHT CREATURES
The bats inhabiting the caves beneath Wayne Manor filled young Bruce with horror.

SECRET PASSAGE
Access to the Batcave from Wayne Manor was through a concealed doorway behind the grandfather clock in Bruce's study. Turning the clock's hands to 10:47 – the exact time of the murders of Thomas and Martha Wayne – opened the hidden passage.

TO FOUR-YEAR-OLD Bruce Wayne, the labyrinthine limestone caverns beneath the Wayne Estate were a place of fear. One day he stumbled and fell into one of these grottoes. He remained trapped with the hundreds of bats nesting there until his father descended into the darkness to rescue him. As an adult, Bruce returned to the cave to establish a subterranean sanctuary for his own bat-inspired alter-ego. Hidden beneath Wayne Manor, this highly-equipped, multipurpose "Batcave" served as the perfect headquarters for the Dark Knight to wage his clandestine war on crime!

Stairway to Wayne Manor

Ballistics analysis

Electron microscope

DNA Spectrograph

Bat-costume vault

Elevator

Hydraulic turntable

World globe

Hats

The Monk's hood

Malay penguin

Judge Clay's gavel

Sword

Jason Todd's costume

Jo... ca...

Dana Drye's diary

Thomas Wayne's "Batman" costume

Two-Face's coin

Giant penny (1947 Lincoln head)

COMPUTER AND WORKSHOP
The Batcave's crime lab and forensics tools rivalled those of the F.B.I. or Interpol. WayneTech sub-contracts had advanced the sciences of genetic and fiber analysis, while quantum leaps in computer engineering provided Batman with the hardware and software necessary to assemble the world's foremost digital database on criminals and their psychology.

THE TROPHY ROOM
Batman's trophies included a robot T. Rex, the diary of detective Dana Drye revealing Bruce Wayne as Batman, the sword of the assassin Deathstroke, the hood of the Monk, a portrait of Bruce (a clue in a past case), the gavel of a crooked judge, and the hats of Tweedledum and Tweedledee.

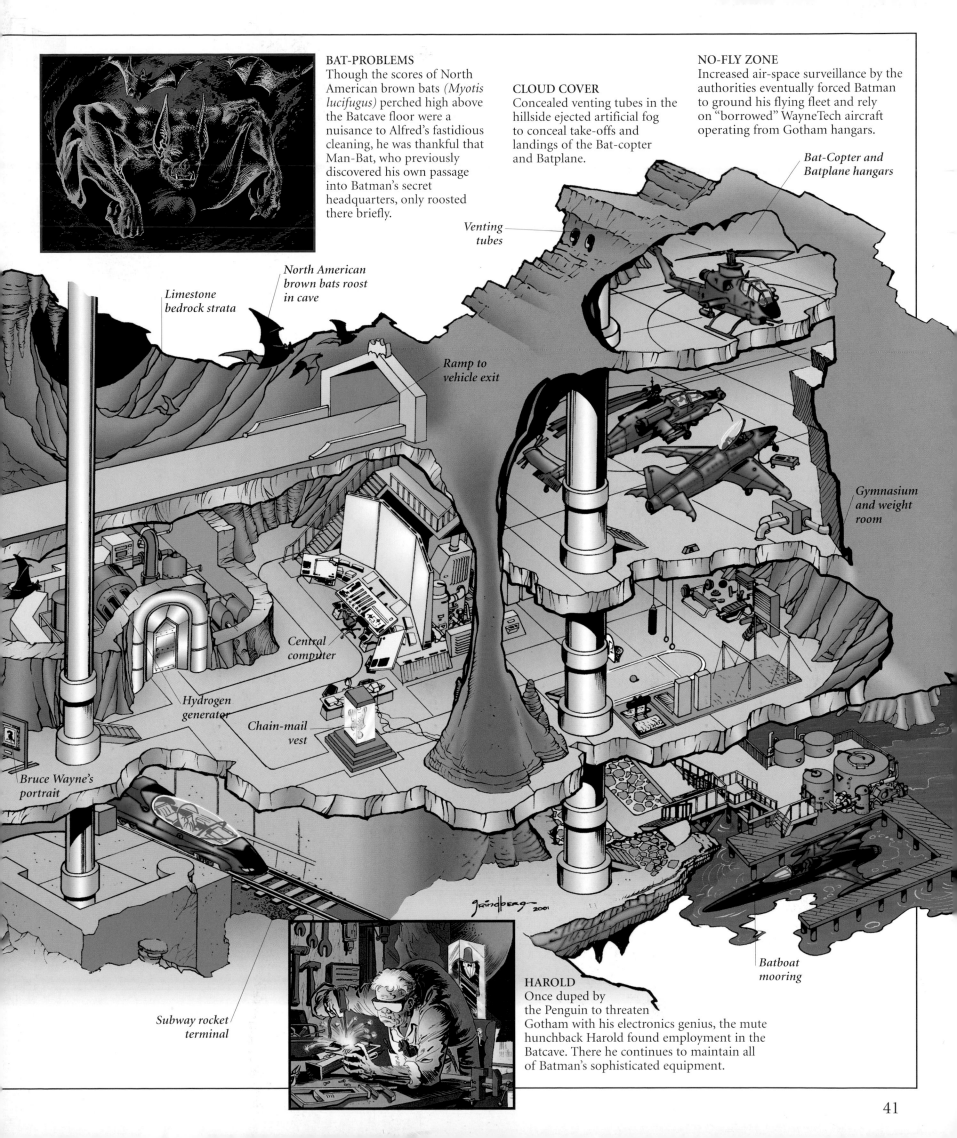

BAT-PROBLEMS
Though the scores of North American brown bats *(Myotis lucifugus)* perched high above the Batcave floor were a nuisance to Alfred's fastidious cleaning, he was thankful that Man-Bat, who previously discovered his own passage into Batman's secret headquarters, only roosted there briefly.

CLOUD COVER
Concealed venting tubes in the hillside ejected artificial fog to conceal take-offs and landings of the Bat-copter and Batplane.

NO-FLY ZONE
Increased air-space surveillance by the authorities eventually forced Batman to ground his flying fleet and rely on "borrowed" WayneTech aircraft operating from Gotham hangars.

Venting tubes

Bat-Copter and Batplane hangars

North American brown bats roost in cave

Limestone bedrock strata

Ramp to vehicle exit

Gymnasium and weight room

Central computer

Hydrogen generator

Chain-mail vest

Bruce Wayne's portrait

Batboat mooring

Subway rocket terminal

HAROLD
Once duped by the Penguin to threaten Gotham with his electronics genius, the mute hunchback Harold found employment in the Batcave. There he continues to maintain all of Batman's sophisticated equipment.

THE NEW BATCAVE

IN THE AFTERMATH of the earthquake that decimated Gotham City and razed the original Batcave, a redesigned headquarters reflects a new era in the Dark Knight's crusade. The rebuilt complex utilizes the cavern's height to greater advantage, with eight separate levels now making up Batman's underground refuge. Amid limestone stalactites and stalagmites, retractable walkways bridge multi-tiered structures, including an "island" computer platform with seven linked Cray T932 mainframes and a state-of-the-art hologram projector. Similar hi-tech updates to training facilities, forensics laboratory, library, and vehicle access have made this re-imagined Batcave a more formidable garrison than ever before.

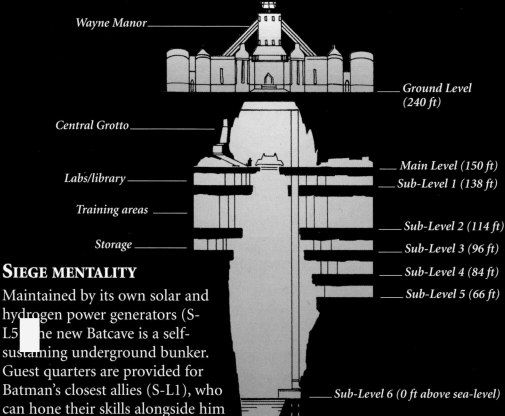

Wayne Manor

Central Grotto

Labs/library

Training areas

Storage

Ground Level (240 ft)

Main Level (150 ft)
Sub-Level 1 (138 ft)

Sub-Level 2 (114 ft)

Sub-Level 3 (96 ft)

Sub-Level 4 (84 ft)

Sub-Level 5 (66 ft)

Sub-Level 6 (0 ft above sea-level)

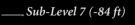

Sub-Level 7 (-84 ft)

SIEGE MENTALITY

Maintained by its own solar and hydrogen power generators (S-L5), the new Batcave is a self-sustaining underground bunker. Guest quarters are provided for Batman's closest allies (S-L1), who can hone their skills alongside him in the improved gymnasium and shooting range (S-L2). As before, the diminutive Harold lives in the cave (S-L4), maintaining the vehicles and equipment, including the Subway Rocket and Batboat (S-L6). Elevator access is provided to all levels, including a submerged chamber far below the water table (S-L5). To date, the purposes of S-L7 are known only to Batman.

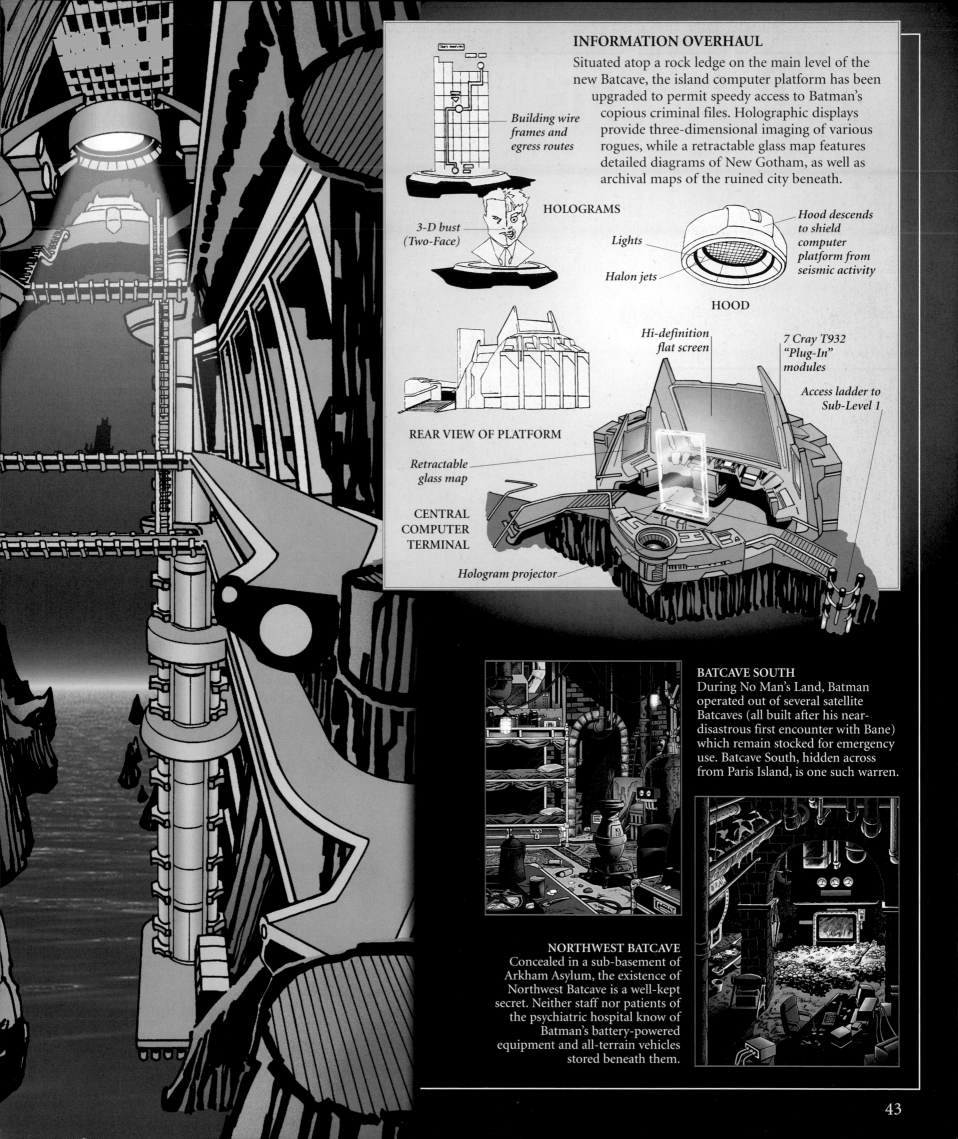

INFORMATION OVERHAUL

Situated atop a rock ledge on the main level of the new Batcave, the island computer platform has been upgraded to permit speedy access to Batman's copious criminal files. Holographic displays provide three-dimensional imaging of various rogues, while a retractable glass map features detailed diagrams of New Gotham, as well as archival maps of the ruined city beneath.

Building wire frames and egress routes

HOLOGRAMS

3-D bust (Two-Face)

Lights

Halon jets

Hood descends to shield computer platform from seismic activity

HOOD

Hi-definition flat screen

7 Cray T932 "Plug-In" modules

REAR VIEW OF PLATFORM

Access ladder to Sub-Level 1

Retractable glass map

CENTRAL COMPUTER TERMINAL

Hologram projector

BATCAVE SOUTH
During No Man's Land, Batman operated out of several satellite Batcaves (all built after his near-disastrous first encounter with Bane) which remain stocked for emergency use. Batcave South, hidden across from Paris Island, is one such warren.

NORTHWEST BATCAVE
Concealed in a sub-basement of Arkham Asylum, the existence of Northwest Batcave is a well-kept secret. Neither staff nor patients of the psychiatric hospital know of Batman's battery-powered equipment and all-terrain vehicles stored beneath them.

43

BATMOBILES

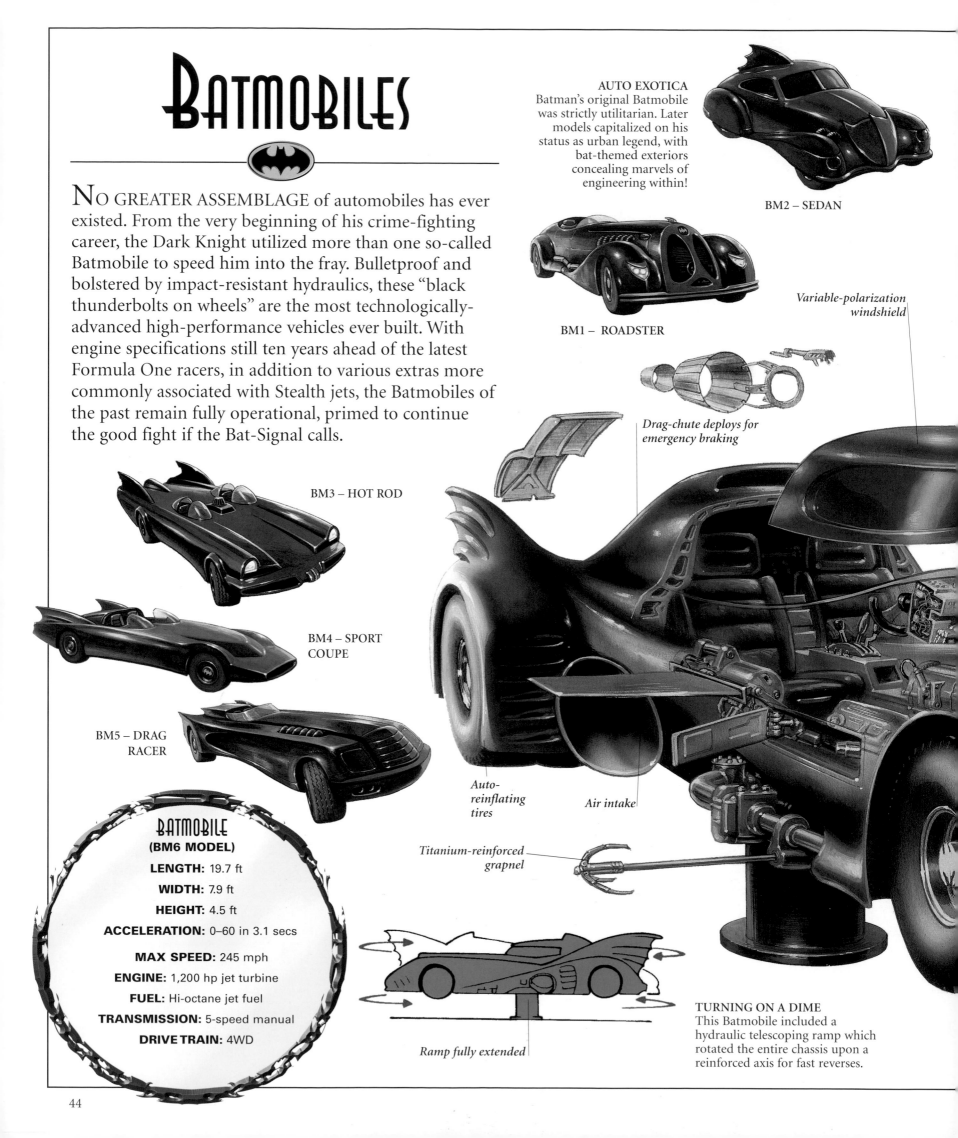

AUTO EXOTICA
Batman's original Batmobile was strictly utilitarian. Later models capitalized on his status as urban legend, with bat-themed exteriors concealing marvels of engineering within!

BM2 – SEDAN

No GREATER ASSEMBLAGE of automobiles has ever existed. From the very beginning of his crime-fighting career, the Dark Knight utilized more than one so-called Batmobile to speed him into the fray. Bulletproof and bolstered by impact-resistant hydraulics, these "black thunderbolts on wheels" are the most technologically-advanced high-performance vehicles ever built. With engine specifications still ten years ahead of the latest Formula One racers, in addition to various extras more commonly associated with Stealth jets, the Batmobiles of the past remain fully operational, primed to continue the good fight if the Bat-Signal calls.

BM1 – ROADSTER

Variable-polarization windshield

Drag-chute deploys for emergency braking

BM3 – HOT ROD

BM4 – SPORT COUPE

BM5 – DRAG RACER

Auto-reinflating tires

Air intake

Titanium-reinforced grapnel

BATMOBILE
(BM6 MODEL)

LENGTH: 19.7 ft

WIDTH: 7.9 ft

HEIGHT: 4.5 ft

ACCELERATION: 0–60 in 3.1 secs

MAX SPEED: 245 mph

ENGINE: 1,200 hp jet turbine

FUEL: Hi-octane jet fuel

TRANSMISSION: 5-speed manual

DRIVE TRAIN: 4WD

Ramp fully extended

TURNING ON A DIME
This Batmobile included a hydraulic telescoping ramp which rotated the entire chassis upon a reinforced axis for fast reverses.

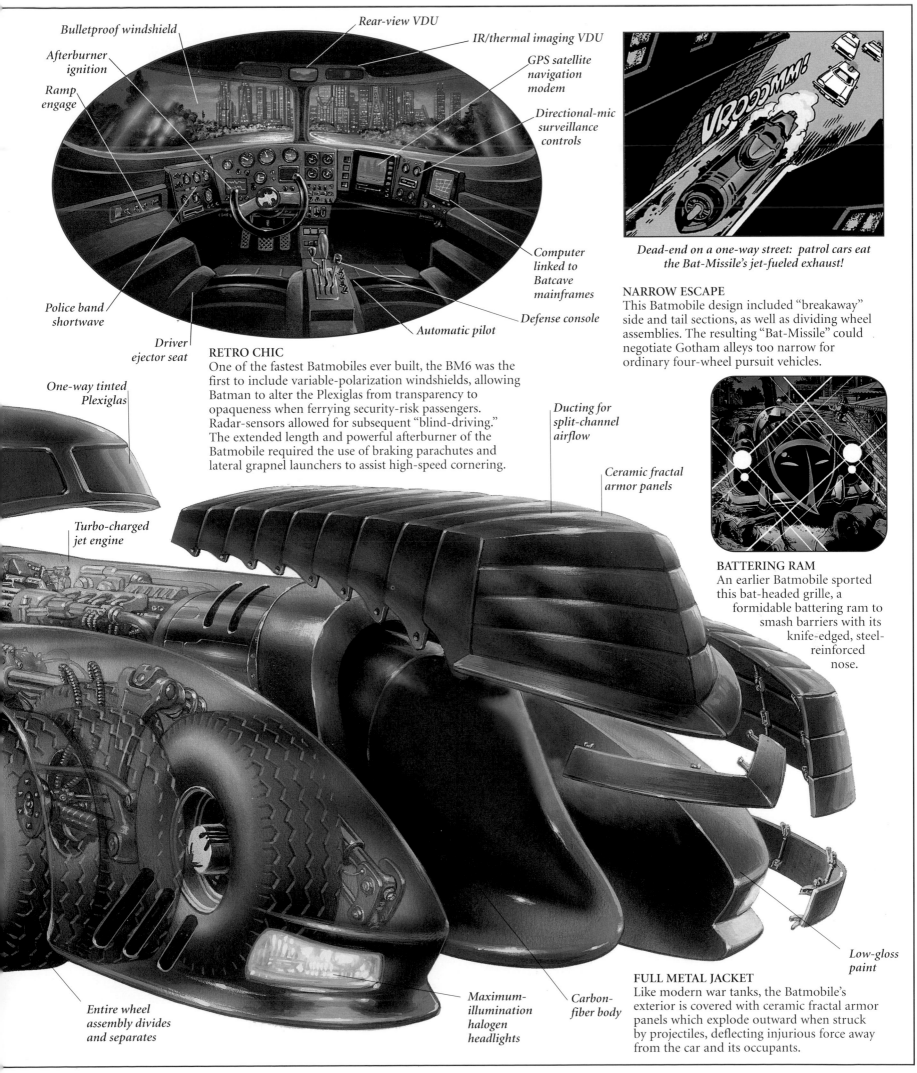

Bulletproof windshield

Afterburner
ignition

Ramp
engage

Police band
shortwave

Driver
ejector seat

Rear-view VDU

IR/thermal imaging VDU

GPS satellite
navigation
modem

Directional-mic
surveillance
controls

Computer
linked to
Batcave
mainframes

Defense console

Automatic pilot

One-way tinted
Plexiglas

Turbo-charged
jet engine

Dead-end on a one-way street: patrol cars eat
the Bat-Missile's jet-fueled exhaust!

NARROW ESCAPE
This Batmobile design included "breakaway"
side and tail sections, as well as dividing wheel
assemblies. The resulting "Bat-Missile" could
negotiate Gotham alleys too narrow for
ordinary four-wheel pursuit vehicles.

RETRO CHIC
One of the fastest Batmobiles ever built, the BM6 was the
first to include variable-polarization windshields, allowing
Batman to alter the Plexiglas from transparency to
opaqueness when ferrying security-risk passengers.
Radar-sensors allowed for subsequent "blind-driving."
The extended length and powerful afterburner of the
Batmobile required the use of braking parachutes and
lateral grapnel launchers to assist high-speed cornering.

Ducting for
split-channel
airflow

Ceramic fractal
armor panels

BATTERING RAM
An earlier Batmobile sported
this bat-headed grille, a
formidable battering ram to
smash barriers with its
knife-edged, steel-
reinforced
nose.

Entire wheel
assembly divides
and separates

Maximum-
illumination
halogen
headlights

Carbon-
fiber body

Low-gloss
paint

FULL METAL JACKET
Like modern war tanks, the Batmobile's
exterior is covered with ceramic fractal armor
panels which explode outward when struck
by projectiles, deflecting injurious force away
from the car and its occupants.

WHEELS OF THE BAT

TO THE DARK KNIGHT, it is simply "The Car." But on the mean streets of Gotham City, the Batmobile has become the stuff of urban legend to the unfortunate criminals who have stared upon its ominous bat-headed grille-work. Modified from the chassis up by Bruce Wayne himself, the current Batmobile is a turbo-charged and armor-plated street fighter specially outfitted for Batman's unrelenting war on crime. Equipped with the latest technology – including several pirated WayneTech prototypes – the Batmobile's versatility as high-speed transport, roving forensics lab, and armored dreadnought has made it an indispensable addition to Batman's crusade.

REAR DEFENSES
Few cars can match the Batmobile for sheer speed and acceleration. Nevertheless, Batman has installed several deterrents to thwart any criminal fool enough to give his vehicle chase. These rear-deployed defenses include high-viscosity, Teflon-based lubricant slicks, blinding smoke-screen clouds, and tire-piercing caltrops.

CURRENT MODEL

More so than any previous design, the Dark Knight's current Batmobile is by far the swiftest and most agile of its kind, as well as the most self-reliant. Auto-engaged twin auxiliary fuel-tanks increase the Batmobile's already considerable range, while seven-day emergency rations and water stores in the trunk allow for journeys outside of Gotham City if necessity demands an extended road-trip.

Ceramic-composite exterior

Variable-polarization windshield

WHEELS
The Batmobile's gel-filled Kevlar-reinforced tires are puncture-proof and flame-resistant with pressure regulated by dashboard controls. Tire over-inflation extrudes imbedded studs in all-weather treads for extra grip on icy roads.

Rear-wheel independent drive

Adhesive-trap foam gun

Aerosolized regurgitant sprayer

Digital wheel locks

Anti-lock double-disc brakes

STICKY FOAM
The adhesive-trap foam gun shoots non-toxic liquid resin (stabilized under pressure), which expands into a gelatinous, sticky lather upon contact with the air.

BATMOBILE
(BM7 MODEL)

LENGTH: 16.6 ft

WIDTH: 6.4 ft **HEIGHT:** 4.8 ft

MAX. SPEED: 266 mph

ACCELERATION: 0-60 in 2.4 secs

ENGINE: 1,500 hp jet turbine

FUEL: Gasoline/ethanol mix

TRANSMISSION:
6-speed manual

ABSOLUTE CONTROL
The fully-automated Batmobile may be operated by voice-command radio links in Batman's cowl, as well as by a limited-function, hand-held key-pad and Remote System Controller.

BAT-HUMVEE
When the Cataclysm destroyed Gotham's infrastructure, Batman took to the rubble-strewn streets in a custom HMMWV with 6.5-liter diesel/gas engine, raised suspension, and variable-pressure all-terrain tires.

Bulletproof wind-guard

Computer-controlled carburetor

BAT-CYCLE
For the benefit of his "family" of associate crime-fighters, Batman maintains several specialized motorcycles. The Dark Knight's personal Bat-Cycle is a modified street-bike with a 786 cc liquid-cooled V-4 engine.

Rocket-fired ejector seats

Side-impact air-bags

Triple-stage afterburner

Gel-filled tires

Twin-screw supercharger

1,500 hp gas/turbine engine

COMMUNICATIONS
The Batmobile's dashboard computer is linked to the Batcave via a cellular modem. Its back-scoop conceals a satellite dish for TV/radio/GPS linkage. Other features include speed-measuring radar, landsat video mapper, police band monitor, and controls for external loudspeakers.

ANTI-THEFT DEVICES
If Batman is incapacitated or rendered unconscious, the Batmobile initiates a five-tier defense system to protect both its driver and itself. *Phase 1:* Proximity alarms enact lock-down and surface electrification. *Phase 2:* Regurgitant gas deployed in immediate proximity while recorded SOS is relayed to Batcave. *Phase 3:* Hypersonic trilling spheres are released. *Phase 4:* Motion-tracking glue nozzles eject super-adhesive foam. *Phase 5:* The Batmobile self-destructs!

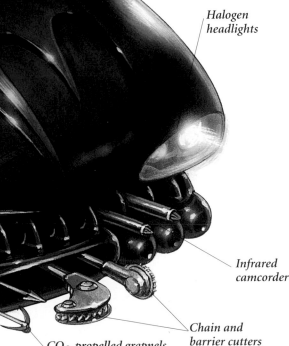

Halogen headlights

Infrared camcorder

Floodlights

CO_2-propelled grapnels

Chain and barrier cutters

WINGS OF THE BAT

THE DARK KNIGHT SOARS on wings of steel. With the extraordinary wealth and technological resources of Bruce Wayne's industrial companies at his disposal, the Batman has assembled a small fleet of vehicles designed to carry him high above Gotham City's crime-infested streets. From stealthy leather-winged hang-gliders and collapsible single-occupant "Whirly-bats" carried in the trunk of the Batmobile, to fully-outfitted attack helicopters and VTOL-converted corporate jets, the Dark Knight takes full advantage of WayneTech patents and military contracts to ensure unsurpassed air-superiority over Gotham.

ON BORROWED WINGS

Batman once maintained aircraft in his original Batcave, although launching these vehicles so close to Wayne Manor's neighboring estates threatened to compromise his secret identity. The Dark Knight now "borrows" specially-modified jets and helicopters from Wayne Aerospace's business and military contracts. A few very specific craft remain fueled and ready for Bruce Wayne's private use, no questions asked.

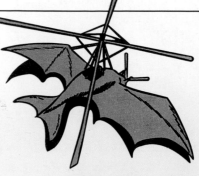

VERTICAL LIMIT
Realizing the value of VTOL (Vertical Take-Off/Landing) capabilities, Batman once built this scalloped-winged helicopter/turboprop Bat-Gyro. It was later mothballed as too slow and unwieldy.

BAT-GYRO

BAT-PLANE I

JET PROPULSION
Batplane I and the Bat-Rocket favored Batman's signature look over sleek aerodynamics. Batplane II, a retooled Wayne Aerospace W4 Wraith fighter, married style with substance.

BAT-ROCKET

BATPLANE II

STAGE 3 – SUB-ORBITAL
Gaining further altitude (45,000-55,000 ft), delta fins in tail and snub winglets elongate to increase efficiency and stability as speeds approach supersonic.

STAGE 2 – CONVERSION
At cruising altitude (35,000-45,000 ft), telescoping wings retract. Exterior sections of tail and nose-cone envelop cockpit and cabin fuselage for higher altitude pressurization.

BAT-GLIDER
This highly steerable para-glider, featuring Kevlar-braced struts and magnesium alloy hinging, folds into a shoulder-slung case. The central spar includes a flotation device and a water-activated emergency beacon with radio and strobe light.

STAGE 1 – TAKEOFF
Batplane III, a modified Wayne Aviation SlipStream ($46 million sans "extras"), is detailed to resemble a standard mid-size corporate jet during take-offs and landings.

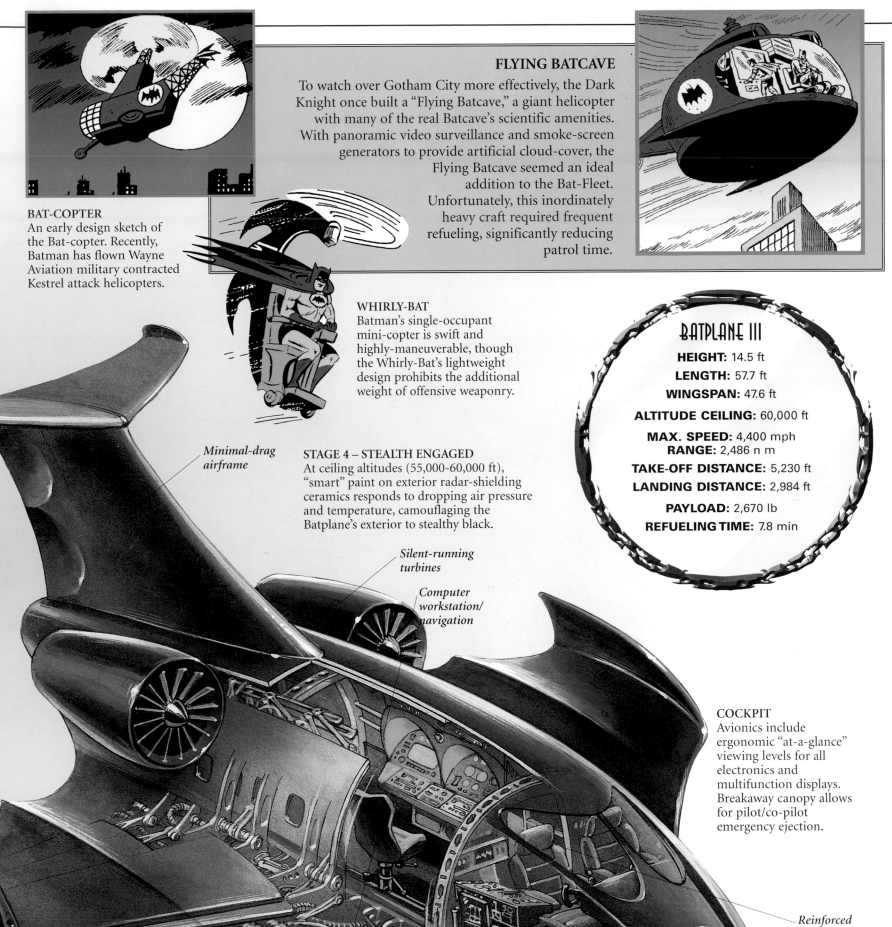

BAT-COPTER
An early design sketch of the Bat-copter. Recently, Batman has flown Wayne Aviation military contracted Kestrel attack helicopters.

FLYING BATCAVE
To watch over Gotham City more effectively, the Dark Knight once built a "Flying Batcave," a giant helicopter with many of the real Batcave's scientific amenities. With panoramic video surveillance and smoke-screen generators to provide artificial cloud-cover, the Flying Batcave seemed an ideal addition to the Bat-Fleet. Unfortunately, this inordinately heavy craft required frequent refueling, significantly reducing patrol time.

WHIRLY-BAT
Batman's single-occupant mini-copter is swift and highly-maneuverable, though the Whirly-Bat's lightweight design prohibits the additional weight of offensive weaponry.

Minimal-drag airframe

STAGE 4 – STEALTH ENGAGED
At ceiling altitudes (55,000-60,000 ft), "smart" paint on exterior radar-shielding ceramics responds to dropping air pressure and temperature, camouflaging the Batplane's exterior to stealthy black.

Silent-running turbines

Computer workstation/ navigation

BATPLANE III
HEIGHT: 14.5 ft
LENGTH: 57.7 ft
WINGSPAN: 47.6 ft
ALTITUDE CEILING: 60,000 ft
MAX. SPEED: 4,400 mph
RANGE: 2,486 n m
TAKE-OFF DISTANCE: 5,230 ft
LANDING DISTANCE: 2,984 ft
PAYLOAD: 2,670 lb
REFUELING TIME: 7.8 min

COCKPIT
Avionics include ergonomic "at-a-glance" viewing levels for all electronics and multifunction displays. Breakaway canopy allows for pilot/co-pilot emergency ejection.

Reinforced Plexiglass canopy windows polarize at stealth altitude

Wings protected by bleed-air anti-icing system

Cabin capacity for up to six passengers

BAT-VEHICLES

COCKPIT
The Batboat's displays include state-of-the-art navigation and communication links, ascent-rate alarm, dive-time clock, and safe-ceiling depth meter.

SOMETIMES A CAR just isn't enough. When crime descends beneath Gotham City's streets or spills into its surrounding waterways, the Dark Knight employs other modes of high-powered transportation uniquely suited to the situation. Sub-Level 4 of the Batcave houses a Subway Rocket linking directly to the Gotham Metro tunnel system via secret annexes recorded on no city plans. Even further below, in Sub-Level 6, is moored an aqua-dynamic hydrofoil/submersible, a "Batboat" at home on both the navigable Gotham River and the waters of the Atlantic Ocean.

Tail-fin serves as rudder when submerged

Jet engine

DIVE MASTER
With Gotham Harbor a confluence of aquatic smuggling, Batman has become an accomplished diver.

HYDROFOIL
To submerge, the Batboat's foils retract to reduce parasitic drag. Its aluminum propellers are driven by sealed AH electrolyte batteries.

Vibration-minimal propulsion

Advanced composite alloy

BAT-STRIKE
Neutral-buoyancy undersea scooter with submerged speeds in excess of 5 knots.

Cockpit de-pressurizes for scuba egress

Baffles seal exhaust ports watertight

Reinforced poly-acrylic canopy

SUBWAY ROCKET

Designed and built by Harold, the Batcave's engineer-in-residence, the Subway Rocket was first utilized by Jean-Paul Valley during his tumultuous tenure as Dark Knight. This jet-propelled rail car provides access to downtown Gotham in mere minutes. Navigational systems divert the Rocket from oncoming passenger trains, while an onboard jamming device cloaks it from Gotham Transit Authority's tracking computers.

BAT-SUBMERSIBLE
Environment systems include CO_2-scrubbers and air-conditioning units in Bat-Submersible's stern. Oxygen tanks provide up to 6 hours of breathable air, with emergency tanks allowing an added 12 hours of life-support, including oxygen/helium mixes for deep-water submersion.

BATBOAT

LENGTH: 25.4 ft

BEAM: 8.6 ft

HULL TYPE: Catamaran

MAX. SURFACE SPEED: 120 mph (standard)/150 mph (hydrofoil)

MAX. SUBMERGED SPEED: 30 knots

MAX. DEPTH: Guaranteed to 200 ft

Two-person cockpit

Variable-ballast tanks in pontoon

Vacuum-bagged Kevlar-composite hull

Harpoon gun

Lateral thrusters

Retractable grapnel/anchor

Radar/sonar and GPS arrays in bow

Depth charge

Active-homing torpedo

GOING OVERBOARD

Early in his career, Batman investigated arms dealers operating along the wharves of Gotham's Chinatown district. Pursuing the fleeing criminals in a prototype Batboat, the Dark Knight destroyed their launch with a bow-mounted flame-thrower, an "extreme measure" he later abandoned.

OFFENSIVE WEAPONS

Batboat armaments include a pneumatic harpoon with high-tensile titanium cable, a launching grapnel that doubles as an anchor, variable-setting depth charges, and a small supply of active-homing torpedoes with heat/motion/vibration target-acquisition.

Allies of the Bat

THE DARK KNIGHT'S LONE VIGIL was not to last. From the very start, Bruce Wayne trusted a scant few with the details of his secret life. His stalwart valet Alfred would be the first, witness to the birth of the Batman following the tragedy befalling young Bruce's beloved parents in Crime Alley. But as time and his crusade wore on, Bruce realized that others shared his deeply abiding hunger for justice. Orphaned circus aerialist Dick Grayson would soon become his squire, proving both an able partner and a bolt of optimism in a seemingly endless struggle. Even the daughter of James Gordon, the Dark Knight's single proponent within Gotham City's Police Department, would find inspiration in the shadow of the Bat, donning her own cape and cowl. And still there would be more, men and women just like Bruce, lost youths drawn inexorably to a higher and more noble calling. What began as a solitary campaign is now a united front in the war on crime, a small army of selfless vigilantes pledging devoted service to Batman and his cause.

Alfred

HE WAS THERE from the very start. Valet and gentleman's gentleman to the wealthy Wayne family, Alfred Pennyworth provided staunch support to young Bruce Wayne when his parents were murdered. It was Alfred who abetted Bruce in convincing Gotham's social services to keep the boy out of foster care. It was Alfred who enabled the driven youth to immerse himself in the training necessary to carry out his personal crusade. And to this day, it is Alfred who remains a steadfast friend and surrogate father to the Dark Knight and his squires, salving their wounds, mending their costumes, and proffering sage counsel when they need it most.

ARE YOU ALL RIGHT, MASTER BRUCE?

MY MOTHER AND FATHER ARE DEAD... AND MY LIFE FEELS VERY DIFFERENT RIGHT NOW.

YOU ALWAYS SAY THE TRUTH IS BEST, SO I WON'T LIE.

NO... I'M NOT ALL RIGHT.

THEY WERE GOOD... THEY WERE EVERYTHING... BUT THEY'RE GONE.

FATHER FIGURE
Alfred's loyalty runs deep. Yet why he aided Bruce's efforts in embarking on a long and lonely road to retribution remains a mystery. Alfred himself often regrets his complicity in the creation of the Batman.

HELP ME, ALFRED.

I NEED STRENGTH.

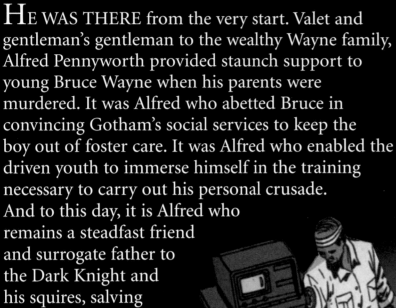

CRITICAL CARE
Alfred has never sworn the Hippocratic Oath, nor does he hold any medical school diploma, though the innumerable broken bones, bullet wounds, and knife slashes he has treated certainly merit an honorary degree. However, his greatest fears were realized when Bane battered the Dark Knight's body far beyond his meager abilities to repair it. As Bruce lay unconscious and near death, Alfred feared the very worst.

Be it soup spoon, scalpel or spot-welder, Alfred wields each with a steady hand.

RENAISSANCE MAN
Erudite and well-traveled, Alfred's duties as valet to Bruce Wayne and aide to Batman have fostered more than a few esoteric talents. Whether concocting exotic soufflés or rebuilding fuel-injected carburetors, Alfred slips effortlessly from role to role, a skill refined during his years as an actor on the London stage.

LONELY HEARTS
Dr. Leslie Thompkins is Alfred's closest association outside of Wayne Manor. Both privy to Bruce's secret, Leslie and Alfred have grown closer in their years mending a broken and bleeding Batman. Over tea and conversation, the two enjoy a tender kiss, before a wounded Dark Knight spoils the mood.

Alfred would gladly offer his life to preserve Batman's secrets, though not without a fight!

> I AM A DEAD SHOT AND THE GREENER IS LOADED WITH DOUBLE-OUGHT.

> SO UNLESS YOU *WISH* TO BE--

UNERRING AIM
Unlike his employer, Alfred has no qualms about taking up firearms to protect his charges, brandishing his Greener shotgun in a vain attempt to halt Bane's siege of Wayne Manor!

> UNNH!

ALFRED

FULL NAME:
Alfred Pennyworth

OCCUPATION: Valet

BASE: Gotham City

HEIGHT: 6 ft **WEIGHT:** 160 lb

EYES: Blue **HAIR:** Black

FIRST APPEARANCE:
BATMAN #16
(April–May, 1943)

DEFENDER OF THE FAITH
Alfred would be the first to admit that life in the shadow of the Bat has been both a blessing and a curse. From the very beginning he has kept journals chronicling the crusade to which he bears witness. These cite every victory over madmen or defeat of monsters with an attention to detail that comes with a fundamental belief in the rightness of Batman's existence. Alfred only hopes to live long enough to see an end to his master's war.

NIGHTWING

THE FLYING GRAYSONS
When Haly's Circus refused to pay protection to racketeer "Boss" Zucco, the Flying Graysons paid the ultimate price when Zucco's gang sabotaged their trapeze lines!

THE DARK KNIGHT would have a squire. When gangster "Boss" Zucco murdered his circus acrobat parents, Dick Grayson found himself under the protective wing of the Batman, who trained him to be Robin, his second in the crusade against injustice. The "Boy Wonder" battled alongside Batman for years until a growing concern for Robin's welfare forced the Dark Knight to dissolve their partnership. Flying solo, Dick continued the good fight into manhood, passing on the guise of Robin to adopt a new secret identity inspired in the shadow of the bat, yet wholly his own: Nightwing!

HEROES IN LOVE
Barbara Gordon (alias Oracle) had long resisted Dick Grayson's ardent feelings for her – despite sharing similar emotions herself. Eventually Dick's persistence won out, and the two are now blissfully in love.

Shatterproof polymer Escrima sticks

THE DYNAMIC DUO
With a one-two punch, the grinning Boy Wonder was the ideal crime-fighting partner. His youthful exuberance buoyed Batman's spirits during the Dark Knight's darkest hours.

MISSED AGAIN!
Batman's grueling training pushed Dick's already lightning-quick reflexes to be faster than the aim of his foes!

BLAM BLAM BLAM
BLAM
BLAM
BLAM

Primer paint "street camouflage" ensures the Nightbird looks like any other car

Starlite night-vision lenses in mask

"Muscle Car" body shell

THE NIGHTBIRD
Nightwing's vehicle includes many of the same hi-tech extras as the Batmobile, in addition to a WayneTech-modified 6,064 cc engine (627 BHP at 7,400 rpm). The vehicle also has chassis locking clamps for interchangeable, carbon-fiber over aluminum endoskeleton body shell "disguises" (taxi, police cruiser, etc).

GAUNTLETS
Instead of a Utility Belt, Nightwing prefers a more economic arsenal concealed throughout eight compartments in his glove gauntlets.

Spare telescoping Escrimas

Hand-held 100,000-volt taser

"Wing-Ding" Mini-Batarang compartment

Self-destruct cuff charges

BLÜD RIVALS
Nightwing thought he could school Tad "Nite-Wing" Ryerstad in the finer points of crime-fighting. Instead, this erstwhile apprentice murdered F.B.I. agent Cisco Blaine, forcing Nightwing to take down his former pupil.

PRODIGAL SON
For a brief time, Dick assumed the mantle of the Bat, conquering his fear of the murderous Two-Face and proving to both himself and his mentor that he was the only choice to succeed Bruce Wayne as Batman.

NIGHTWING

REAL NAME:
Richard "Dick" Grayson

OCCUPATION: Police Officer

BASE: Blüdhaven

HEIGHT: 5 ft 10 in **WEIGHT:** 175 lb

EYES: Blue **HAIR:** Black

FIRST APPEARANCE:
DETECTIVE COMICS #38
(April, 1940)

BLÜDHAVEN

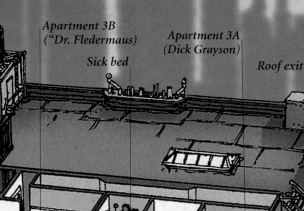

POSTCARD FROM AVALON
Blüdhaven (incorporated 1912) is bordered to the north by briny marshes. The Avalon River bisecting the commonwealth feeds directly into the Atlantic.

THE ONLY THING DIRTIER than the smog-choked streets of Blüdhaven are the city's cops, most of whom are on the take. Neighboring commonwealth to Gotham City, Blüdhaven began its days as a fairly prosperous whaling port. But as Gotham capitalized on industry and technology to foster its continued growth, neither succeeded in gaining a significant economic foothold in Blüdhaven. While depression has stalled the city's fiscal and moral evolution, vice runs rampant, fed by the entrenched mob presence of Roland Desmond – aka the gargantuan criminal genius Blockbuster – aided and abetted by Blüdhaven's infamous police force, where corruption is the rule, *not* the exception.

1013 PARKTHORNE
Dick Grayson lives at 1013 Parkthorne Avenue. Fellow tenants include landlady and medical student Bridget Clancy, John Law (aka 1940s "Mystery Man" Tarantula), and Aaron Helzinger (former Bat-rogue Amygdala).

THE THIN BLUE LINE

Since Nightwing's midnight raids did no more than destabilize Blockbuster's criminal beachhead in Blüdhaven, Nightwing decided to help the city by day as well, enrolling in the Haven County Police Academy. Though extended unauthorized "absences" marred his otherwise exemplary record, Officer Richard Grayson graduated in the upper 86th percentile of his class. Now on Blüdhaven's daylight beat, Officer Grayson trains with 10-year veteran Amy Rohrbach, while attempting to ferret out the bad cops from the good.

Roof tank

Apartment 3B ("Dr. Fledermaus)

Apartment 3A (Dick Grayson)

Sick bed

Roof exit

Elevator room

Manual elevator

Quick-release window entry

Rapid wall breech building exit

Concealed entry to 3rd floor

Clothes closet

Cmdr. Darren Michaelmas

Officer Richard Grayson

Sgt. Amy Rohrback

NIGHTWING'S AERIE
As secret owner of his apartment building, Dick Grayson has converted the entire 3rd floor into lodgings for himself and "Dr. Fledermaus," his own alter-ego and absentee tenant, allowing Nightwing to come and go as he pleases!

GOOD COP/BAD COP
Blüdhaven's police department has been under scrutiny for decades, with various federal law enforcement agencies investigating rumors of rampant corruption and links to organized crime.

LOCKHAVEN
Since the destruction of the city's holding cells by Dudley Soames, Lockhaven Penitentiary is the overcrowded home to Soames and Tad Ryerstad (aka Nite-Wing), each guarded by corrections officer Aaron Helzinger!

HELLA
Policewoman Kate Riordan was horribly burned in a Mob bombing which killed her entire family of Irish-American cops. With nerve-endings removed and new skin grafted to her body, Riordan exacted her own revenge as Hella.

NITE-WING
Urban thug Tad Ryerstad knew nothing of Blüdhaven's *other* vigilante when the unstable young man took the name Nite-Wing from a 24-hour deli specializing in spicy chicken wings.

TORQUE
Corrupt police inspector Dudley "Deadly" Soames had his neck wrenched 180-degrees by Blockbuster — hence his nickname "Torque." Radical drug therapy saved his life but left him horribly deformed… and yearning for vengeance.

BLOCKBUSTER
Roland Desmond is as intimidating for his sheer physical bulk as for his unmatched criminal intellect. With shrewd manipulation, Blockbuster ousted Blüdhaven crime boss Angel Marin and fended off Black Mask's minions to keep a stranglehold on Blüdhaven… the first step in his campaign to dominate Gotham City itself!

DEATH OF ROBIN

HE WAS A GOOD SOLDIER. But despite undertaking as rigorous a training regimen as his predecessor Dick Grayson, the rebellious Jason Todd lacked the maturity to function effectively as Batman's junior partner. That would prove his undoing. In a quest to find his real mother, the troubled orphan journeyed with his mentor to Ethiopia, where they met Dr. Sheila Haywood… *and* the Clown Prince of Crime! Ignoring the Dark Knight's explicit orders, Robin tackled the Joker alone. Betrayed by his own mother, Jason was savagely beaten and left to die with her in a warehouse wired to explode! Tragically, Batman would discover the reunited mother and son's lifeless bodies in the rubble. This time, unfortunately, the Joker had WON.

TIRE THIEF
Batman first met Jason stealing tires off the Batmobile!

> ROBIN !! WHAT DO YOU THINK YOU'RE DOING?!

> WHAT I WAS TRAINED TO DO!

> GONNA KICK SOME TAIL !!

RUSHING IN
In direct defiance of his mentor, Jason leapt into the fray!

THE SEARCH IS OVER

In a trek across the Middle East, Jason ultimately met his real mother in a refugee camp amid the drought-scorched soils of Magdala, Ethiopia. There, Dr. Sheila Haywood attempted in vain to atone for the sins of her youth by providing famine relief. Haywood never thought that the past and the son she had abandoned would one day catch up with her.

THE LAST LAUGH
The Joker's revenge for past defeats was swift, brutal, and final. After his hired thugs had weakened the Boy Wonder, the Clown Prince of Crime attacked Robin with a crowbar, thrashing him mercilessly while his mother watched.

A DEATH IN THE FAMILY

He was too late. After halting the distribution of medicines poisoned by the Joker, Batman raced back to the medical supply warehouse, only to see it consumed in a blazing fireball. With her dying breath, Dr. Haywood revealed to the Dark Knight that Jason had shielded her from the brunt of the blast. A short distance away, Robin lay dead… a hero 'til the very end.

> JASON!!

> YOU'RE STILL ALIVE!!

NO ESCAPE

With scant minutes to spare on the Joker's time-bomb, Jason's love for the mother he had never known provided strength enough to free her before he succumbed to his terrible injuries. Full of remorse, Dr. Haywood refused to leave her son behind. But to her horror, Haywood discovered that the Joker had locked the door. His warehouse was a death-trap!

ROBIN

![Batman logo]

PARENTAL CONCERNS
Tim's parents – father Jack and stepmother Dana – fear that their son's nocturnal absences run more to juvenile delinquency than heroism.

TIM DRAKE KNEW *THE SECRET*. In the wake of Jason Todd's death, Tim – a youth who had deduced the true identities of Batman and Robin – realized that the increasingly unhinged and withdrawn Dark Knight needed a new squire to give him hope in the face of hopelessness. As the third Robin, Tim has filled that role admirably, but not without struggling to balance his own life with the confidences he now shares. Though unquestionably devoted to his duties to the Batman, Tim nevertheless wonders how previous Robins juggled the pressures of being teenagers, while coping with the perils of this very unorthodox "after-school job."

Starlite lenses, radio receiver/transceiver, and inertial navigation unit concealed in mask

First-aid kit and other supplies stored in sleeve pouches

MINI-COMPUTER
Robin's mini-modem is linked to the Batcave Crays via encrypted WayneTech satellite relays.

High-resolution monitor

Touch-sensitive keypad

Sound and display controls

Detachable R-insignia shuriken

BRENTWOOD ACADEMY
To curb Tim's late-night wanderings, Jack Drake enrolled his son in Bristol's prestigious Brentwood Academy. With a student body of fortunate sons and heirs to foreign lands, this all-boys prep school also caters to the "problem children" of the upper crust, all watched over by strict disciplinarian Dean Vernon Nederlander and his ever-present pug Cardigan.

THE SPOILER
When Tim began his romance with Stephanie Brown, aka The Spoiler, he refused to compromise his secret identity!

LOST LOVE
Tim's first serious girlfriend was Russian emigrée Ariana Dzerchenko, for whom he still has strong feelings.

LICENSED TO DRIVE

Robin's primary vehicle is the swift Redbird, a camouflaged sport coupé with all the armaments of the Batmobile, in addition to polarizing windows and exterior sliding bulletproof conversion panels. Tim also utilizes a modified 491cc, liquid-cooled "motocross" Bat-Cycle.

ROBIN'S TUNIC
Outfitted by Batman for optimum protection, Tim's red-breasted tunic is fire-resistant and Kevlar-shielded with the highest ballistics-rating currently available.

Steel gorget in collar

Nomex outer layer

Lead-weighted tip

Nomex fire-resistant material

ROBIN'S CAPE
This is also Nomex and Kevlar interwoven to be fire-resistant and bulletproof. Its weighted ends may be used for offensive purposes.

Quick-release hasp with self-destruct mechanism

Triple-weave Kevlar body armor

UTILITY BELT
In addition to Batman's standard complement, Tim's Utility Belt includes a storage sheath for his telescoping Bo staff, slingshot, exploding Bang-a-rangs, and various computer hacker tools.

Rechargeable oxygen cylinder

Gas pellet pouch

Removable buckle reveals mouthpiece/ purge valve

Emergency rebreather with 15 minutes of breathing time per oxygen cylinder

Unlike the "pixie shoes" of previous Robins, Tim wears split-toe ninja tabi boots for stealth and added traction

ROBIN

REAL NAME: Timothy Drake

OCCUPATION: Student

BASE: Bristol Commons

HEIGHT: 5 ft 1 in **WEIGHT:** 115 lb

EYES: Blue **HAIR:** Black

FIRST APPEARANCE:
BATMAN #436 (August, 1989)
As Robin: BATMAN #457
(December, 1990)

SPOILER

DON'T EVER CALL Stephanie Brown a "Daddy's Girl." Daughter of Arthur Brown, aka the Cluemaster, Stephanie has spent her life in shame of her felonious father. Tiring of his endless empty promises, Stephanie decided to spoil Cluemaster's latest crime spree by donning a costume of her own and "clueing in" Batman and Robin to Brown's schemes. But even after Cluemaster returned to Blackgate Penitentiary for rehabilitation, "The Spoiler" remained active as a nocturnal vigilante, despite the Dark Knight's vocal disapproval. And of even greater concern to Batman was the growing affection between Stephanie and a certain Teen Wonder, who has tried in vain to convince her to forsake the masked life.

FAMILY TIES

Previously, the Spoiler acted without Batman's official endorsement. Times have changed. When Batman was unable to locate Robin (who was missing in the Himalayas), he sought Stephanie Brown's help. The concerned Dark Knight even revealed his partner's secret identity to Stephanie, much to Robin's later dismay. Realizing that she fully intended to continue her course as the Spoiler, Batman has taken Stephanie under his wing, where he can supervise a more formalized training regimen designed to help keep her alive. She is determined not to fail her new mentor.

SECRET LOVE
Robin never planned to fall in love with Stephanie Brown, but the Spoiler was perhaps the only person capable of understanding the dual life of a teen vigilante. Stephanie only hopes that their feelings can endure now that both of their masks are laid bare.

MOTHER KNOWS BEST
Crystal Brown vehemently disapproves of her daughter's extracurricular activities and would much prefer that Stephanie exercise her above-average gymnastic skills anywhere else than high above Gotham City's mean streets.

Util.

Regurgi
capsule

BORROWED TOYS
Spoiler's arsenal of Flash/Bang capsules was formerly supplied by Robin. With access to the Batcave, her bag of tricks has been substantially improved.

CLUELESS
Arthur Brown has always been a second-rate rogue. Copying the methods of the Riddler, Brown dubbed himself "Cluemaster" and staged elaborate robberies predicated by complex clues, which invariably led to his capture. After years of defeat, he has finally gotten the hint.

FIGHT OR FLIGHT
Once preferring diversion to open combat, Spoiler is now being rigorously schooled by the Dark Knight in martial arts. Frequently, Batgirl is her sparring partner.

SPOILER

REAL NAME:
Stephanie Brown

OCCUPATION: High School Student

BASE: Gotham Heights

HEIGHT: 5 ft 5 in **WEIGHT:** 110 lb

EYES: Blue **HAIR:** Blonde

FIRST APPEARANCE:
DETECTIVE COMICS #647
(August, 1992)

BAT-CONCERNS
Initially, Batman worried that Stephanie's vendetta against her father might lead her in the same violent footsteps as another daughter of crime, the Huntress.

THE CHOICE
In the aftermath of the Cataclysm, Stephanie became pregnant by an ex-boyfriend. Faced with an uncertain future for both herself and the child, she chose the heroic path. Her courage bolstered by Robin's comfort, Stephanie allowed the baby to be adopted by a loving adult couple.

SPOILS OF WAR
Spoiler's Utility Belt contains many of the same weapons used by Batman and Robin, including various gas capsules, de-cel jumplines, and Batarangs. Her costume is now Kevlar-reinforced, with Starlite night-vision lenses and a radio comm-link added to her cowl.

elt

ORACLE

THE JOKER'S BULLET would forever define Barbara Gordon. With the Dark Knight as inspiration, Barbara once took to Gotham City's crime-ridden streets as Batgirl, an identity she managed to keep secret from her father, Police Commissioner James Gordon. Though earning Batman's admiration as a frequent partner, Barbara would face her greatest struggle in semi-retirement, when the Clown Prince of Crime shot her through the spine as a prelude to kidnapping the Commissioner. Paralyzed from the waist down, the once high-flying Batgirl refused to let a wheelchair confine her. Unfettered in the cyber-world, Barbara adopted a new guise, using her unparalleled computer expertise to continue the good fight as the all-knowing and all-seeing Oracle!

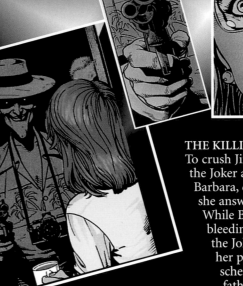

THE KILLING JOKE
To crush Jim Gordon's spirit, the Joker aimed straight at Barbara, crippling her as she answered the door. While Barbara lay bleeding upon the carpet, the Joker photographed her paralyzed body in a scheme to drive her father mad with grief!

BATGIRL
Though she created Batgirl to surprise her father at the Policemen's Masquerade Ball, Barbara put the costume to better use protecting Bruce Wayne from the Killer Moth!

BRAIN BYTES
Gifted with eidetic memory – almost total recall of everything she has ever read or seen – Barbara was once Administrator of the Gotham City Public Library.

Babs goes undercover in civilian guise

DATA CENTRAL

Barbara Gordon's wheelchair has no handles, a signal to all those around her that she is neither helpless nor defenseless. A formidable opponent before her crippling injury, Barbara engages in grueling physical therapy to remain in peak physical condition, relying on her upper body strength for self-defense. But information is Barbara's true weapon, wielded from ever-expanding archives stored in her fortified and wheelchair-accessible headquarters, Gotham City's historic Clocktower.

ORACLE

REAL NAME:
Barbara Gordon

OCCUPATION: Information Broker

BASE: Gotham City

HEIGHT: 5 ft 11 in **WEIGHT:** 126 lb

EYES: Blue **HAIR:** Red

FIRST APPEARANCE:
DETECTIVE COMICS #359
(January, 1967)

THE FLYING TRAPEZE
More than any other sensation, Barbara misses the feeling of flight just before a jumpline is pulled taut. As owner of Haly's Circus, Dick Grayson offered the next best thing on the swinging trapeze high above the sawdust floor of the big top. For a short time, Batgirl soared again, a memory Barbara will always cherish.

THE CLOCKTOWER
Oracle's workstation is comprised of six Yale super-computers sequenced through a 5th-generation interface slaved to her voice-patterns. A sophisticated VR room with holographic heads-up displays provides Oracle with real-time simulations of any location in her database.

THE BLACK CANARY
Oracle employs certain costumed crime-fighters as "field operatives" who respond to crises in global hot spots. Her most frequent partner is Dinah Lance, aka the Black Canary, a founding member of the Justice League of America. Expert in Judo and other martial arts, the Canary also wields her own formidable metahuman-power: a staggering, hyper-pitched, sonic cry.

BATGIRL

HER ONLY LANGUAGE was violence. Adopted daughter of the assassin David Cain – once a sensei of young Bruce Wayne – Cassandra Cain was the ultimate experiment in building the perfect protégée. Denying her verbal stimuli, Cain molded Cassandra into a whisper-quiet combatant, able to read and predict her opponents' attacks with deadly hushed accuracy. But despite her training, Cassandra lacked the stomach for killing. Guilt-ridden over her murder of a Macauan crime kingpin, the mute Cassandra fled from Cain's influence, wandering the globe to elude her father. Ultimately, Cassandra found a higher calling in Gotham City, where she assisted Oracle during the lawlessness of No Man's Land and proved her considerable mettle to the Dark Knight. No longer restricted to silence, Cassandra now wears the mantle of Batgirl as her just reward.

ORIGINAL SIN
Young Cassandra made her first and only kill with her bare hands. Now she risks her own life to atone for that terrible act.

LANGUAGE LESSONS

As a result of her isolated upbringing, the language center of Cassandra's brain had adapted to interpret physical movement as deadly discourse. For Cassandra, vocal communication was virtually impossible until she encountered Jeffers, a powerful psychic on the run from hired killers. With a touch, Jeffers re-ordered Cassandra's thought processes to enable her to understand language and to speak, but at the price of "blinding" her previous skills. To recapture her redoubtable fighting prowess, Cassandra began accelerated re-training, including accepting a costly lesson from assassin Lady Shiva for which she may one day pay dearly.

CHILDREN OF THE BAT
The Huntress lacked the discipline to be the new Batgirl, but for Cassandra Cain, the costume was a perfect fit. As one of Batman's newest pupils, she intends to honor the sacred trust bestowed upon her.

HARRIS
ROYAL

BATGIRL

REAL NAME:
Cassandra Cain

OCCUPATION: Crime Fighter

BASE: Gotham City

HEIGHT: 5 ft 5 in **WEIGHT:** 110 lb

EYES: Brown **HAIR:** Black

FIRST APPEARANCE:
BATMAN #567
(July, 1999)

THAT WAS BEAUTIFUL, BATGIRL, A DANCE, WASN'T IT?

NO?

OH, I GET IT. IT WAS A GIFT! YOUR GIFT TO ME!

SWIFT JUSTICE
At just 17 years old, Batgirl is one of the world's foremost martial artists. Able to predict her foes' moves by reading their body language, Batgirl side-steps any blow, trouncing multiple opponents with ease!

Kevlar-reinforced and Nomex-interwoven costume includes standard-complement utility belt

AZRAEL

TEST-TUBE BABY
After donating her ova to the Order of St. Dumas, Jean Paul's biological mother was to be killed, but a merciful acolyte permitted her to escape. Her identity remains unknown.

BANE OF THE BAT
Haunted by macabre visions of St. Dumas, Jean Paul became an even darker Knight than his predecessor. With "The System" driving him on, Jean Paul redesigned the Bat-Suit, transforming it into Azrael-inspired armor in order to vanquish the venom-fueled Bane!

HOLY WARRIORS Established in the 14th century, the Order of St. Dumas began as a small legion of clergy outside of Papal influence who swore to visit "wrath upon the infidels."

THE DESTINY OF JEAN PAUL VALLEY was writ centuries before his birth. Scientifically altered by the ancient Order of St. Dumas, Jean Paul was molded to be the Order's avenging angel Azrael. With Batman's help, Jean Paul defected from St. Dumas, eventually taking up the Dark Knight's armor when the hero's back was broken by the vile Bane.

Too unstable for the role of grim urban vigilante, Jean Paul was forced to relinquish the mantle of the Bat, later embarking on his own crusade to topple the Order of St. Dumas and prove his worthiness once more to the Dark Knight, who now regards Azrael as a trusted Agent of the Bat.

THE SYSTEM

As a developing fetus inside a glass womb, Jean Paul's brain and blood chemistry were genetically intermingled with animal fluids to enable greatly enhanced strength and agility. Upon his decanting, Jean Paul was further augmented by "The System," an arcane mix of physical and psychological training through hypnotic suggestion. Previously, donning the armor of Azrael triggered the transformation from the passive Jean Paul to the aggressive Azrael. However, Jean Paul has now broken the Order's conditioning by tapping into an even greater strength – his own free will.

AVENGING ARMOR
Jean Paul's original raiment denoted obedience to St. Dumas. A second costume showed fealty to Batman. But his current armor marks a new chapter in the saga of Azrael.

ACQUAINTANCES
Once loyal to St. Dumas, Sister Lilhy now lays claim to the Order's remaining wealth and power. The dwarfling Nomoz – who revealed "The System" to Jean Paul – has fallen mute since forsaking St. Dumas. Ex-psychiatrist Brian Bryan, a friend to Azrael in troubled times, finds peace operating a free clinic in a renovated Gotham cathedral.

ANGEL OF MERCY
Like another wayward orphan, Azrael has found comfort in the care and company of Dr. Leslie Thompkins.

A NEW ORDER
The avenging assassin now a wandering redeemer, Azrael makes his home north of Gotham in a mountaintop aerie built by the Order of St. Dumas.

AZRAEL

REAL NAME:
Jean Paul Valley

OCCUPATION: Adventurer

BASE: Ossaville

HEIGHT: 6 ft 2 in **WEIGHT:** 210 lb

EYES: Blue **HAIR:** Blond

FIRST APPEARANCE:
BATMAN: SWORD OF AZRAEL
#1 (October, 1992)

Huntress

As SOLE SURVIVING member of a leading Gotham City crime family, Helena Bertinelli is no stranger to deadly force. Her childhood was stained with blood when rival Mafia dons conspired to exterminate the Bertinellis. In time, she would repay the Mafia in kind and pursue Gotham's *Cosa Nostra* with swift and sharp justice from the bolts of a crossbow, favored weapon of the Huntress. Once, seeking the Dark Knight's sanction, the Huntress tempered her violent methods in a vain attempt to win his approval. Those days are over. As the feuding cartels of organized crime re-establish their presence in a rebuilt Gotham, the Huntress searches out new criminal prey to sate her hunger for vengeance.

SHARP SHOOTER
Huntress employs a standard complement of gas capsules and her own stylized Batarangs, but prefers crossbow bolts, throwing knives, and CO_2-propelled "wrist-bow" darts to make sure foes get the point.

DOUBLE LIFE

For years, Helena has battled to dismantle the Gotham mob, taking some satisfaction in the knowledge that the girl who might have lived as a "Mafia Princess" had instead become the harbinger of its destruction. However, she recently learned a dark truth about her path to hatred. As Gotham *Mafioso* perished by crossbow bolts aimed to frame her, Helena discovered that Santo Cassamento – the gangster who commissioned the murders of her family – was really her natural father!

THE FAMILY
Santo Cassamento loved Helena's mother, Maria, sister of mobster Tomaso Panessa. To win Maria and eliminate the Bertinellis, Santo ordered his assassin to "spare the sister" and avoid a war with the Panessas. In bitter irony, the hitman inadvertently killed Maria, leaving Helena alive!

VENGEANCE UNLIMITED
Sent to live with relatives in Sicily following the deaths of her father, mother, and brother, Helena was tormented by dreams of her family's assassin. In time, Helena's cousin Salvatore taught her the Sicilian way: *Omerta*. In the years that followed, Helena learned how to hunt and claim her own retribution when blood cried for blood.

SCHOOL TIES
Though provided for by family wealth, Helena was formerly employed as an English teacher in one of Gotham's inner-city high schools. Unfortunately, extended unauthorized absences led to her dismissal! Whether Helena will ever seek another position remains to be seen.

URBAN ENFORCER

During NML, the Huntress sought to earn Batman's esteem by cloaking herself as a new Batgirl, but was unable and unwilling to follow the Dark Knight's unyielding orders. Though briefly allying with rogue cop Billy Pettit, she redeemed herself in the Batman's eyes when she suffered near-fatal wounds protecting 80 innocent men, women, and children from the Joker.

HUNTED BY THE BAT

Framed for the murders of Gotham mobsters, the Huntress was confronted by Batman and Nightwing. To clear her name, she attempted to escape, accidentally wounding the Dark Knight with a bolt from her crossbow. Despite his injury, Batman forgave her, trusting the Huntress to resolve her dilemma.

QUESTIONS AND ANSWERS

Helena's efforts to absolve herself of guilt in the Mafia murders were aided by Vic Sage, aka the Question, a fellow vigilante who once struggled with his own predilection for violence. United by mutual attraction, Vic hopes that his more contemplative influence can temper Helena's relentless vendetta.

HUNTRESS

REAL NAME:
Helena Rosa Bertinelli

OCCUPATION:
Former High School Teacher

BASE: Gotham City

HEIGHT: 5 ft 11 in **WEIGHT:** 148 lb

EYES: Brown **HAIR:** Black

FIRST APPEARANCE:
THE HUNTRESS #1
(April, 1989)

ROGUES GALLERY

THEY ARE THE WORST Gotham City has to offer. Maniacs, murderers, mobsters, and malcontents, their names live in infamy, a veritable *who's who* of villainy with territorial claims to Gotham and psychotic fixations on the Dark Knight as their nemesis. As Bruce Wayne donned the mantle of the Bat to spark fear in the city's criminals, a new breed of garish and flamboyant felons emerged as violent counterpoint: Joker, Two-Face, Bane, and so many others, with rap sheets and body counts in direct proportion to their madness. Evil *beyond* the core, the foes of Batman's Rogues Gallery exist in absolute opposition to the Dark Knight's crusade. He lives to bring order to Gotham. They dream of chaos inspired by their own peculiar manias, either to make themselves fabulously rich… or simply to fulfill an insatiable lust for mayhem. From padded cells in Arkham Asylum or behind iron bars in Blackgate Penitentiary, they plot their next insidious crime waves… while Batman waits for the inevitable clashes to follow.

ARKHAM ASYLUM

MADNESS REIGNS SUPREME in the Elizabeth Arkham Asylum for the Criminally Insane. Established in 1921, Arkham's history has been punctuated by blood and tragedy. Today, the worst of the Dark Knight's rogues gallery regularly find themselves committed to a madhouse too often demonstrating a "revolving-door" policy on criminal rehabilitation, and unable to exorcise the inner demons driving the Joker, Two-Face, and so many others to acts of inexplicable evil.

MERCEY MANSION
Patients newly committed to Arkham Asylum are greeted with a nightmarish facility that seems hardly conducive to mental health! When Bane demolished the more modern hospital complex, Dr. Jeremiah Arkham was forced to occupy the labyrinthine Mercey Mansion. Located just a few short miles fromGotham's DiAngelo Sewage Treatment Plant, Arkham smells of more than just fear.

ACCOMMODATIONS
The incarceration of Gotham's criminally insane necessitates specialized cells for each inmate. Serial killer Mr. Zsasz requires maximum restraints at all times, while Poison Ivy is kept behind shatterproof Plexiglas to avoid contact with her unique pheromones.

SECURITY PERSONNEL
Arkham's security monitors maximum-risk patients via closed-circuit TV. Batons and side-arms are standard for all guards, while orderlies are permitted tasers and pepper-spray.

MADHOUSE RULES
Following Gotham's horrific earthquake, Dr. Arkham was left utterly alone to guard his crazed charges. To prevent their escape, he sealed the building with steel shutters controlled from his office suite. Meanwhile, the inmates ran amok while food and other supplies dwindled!

DR. JEREMIAH ARKHAM
Psychotherapist Jeremiah Arkham has dedicated his life to curing the dangerously deranged, no doubt to atone for the sins of his uncle, Dr. Amadeus Arkham, founder of the Asylum which bears their surname. The institution's very first patient – Martin "Mad Dog" Hawkins – brutally murdered Amadeus's wife and daughter. Thus, Arkham "treated" Hawkins with an electro-shock therapy execution and was later committed to his own facility, which nephew Jeremiah now governs with mixed results.

CONDITIONAL RELEASE
Rather than see his patients die from starvation inside the quake-isolated Asylum, Arkham offered them freedom, but only if the rogues promised not to return to Gotham. Naturally, they lied!

THE JOKER

HE IS THE CLOWN PRINCE OF CRIME. The Ace of Knaves. The Harlequin of Hate. Preeminent among the Dark Knight's rogues gallery, the Joker is certifiably psychotic, driven to the lunatic fringe by a chemical bath which bleached his skin white, dyed his hair shocking green, and peeled his lips back into a leering scarlet rictus. Accessorized with electrocuting joy-buzzers and acid-spurting boutonnieres, the Joker has reinvented mass-murder and terrorism as comedic chaos. His crimes, however, are no laughing matter. Utterly unrepentant, the Joker has delightedly maimed or killed several of the Batman's closest allies… and would gladly do worse if given the chance.

ORIGINAL SIN
Though his story changes from day to day, details of one possible "origin" suggest that the Joker was formerly a failed comedian coerced into crime after the deaths of his wife and unborn child.

RED HOOD
Disguised as "The Red Hood," the failed comedian's attempts to rob Monarch Playing Cards went awry. Forced to flee from the Batman, he dived into the chemical waste vats of the adjacent Ace Chemical Processing!

DANGEROUS
DO NOT APPROACH

The Joker proudly tops every "Most Wanted" list

CHEMICAL PEALS
Barely surviving his toxic swim, the failed comedian emerged from the chemical sludge reborn as an unhinged and ironic clown determined to drive the world just as crazy as himself!

THE JOKER

REAL NAME: Unknown

OCCUPATION:
Professional Criminal

BASE: Gotham City

HEIGHT: 6 ft 5 in **WEIGHT:** 192 lb

EYES: Green **HAIR:** Green

FIRST APPEARANCE:
BATMAN #1
(Spring, 1940)

RIBALD REVENGE
Catching Jason Todd unawares, the Joker bludgeoned the Boy Wonder and left him to die alongside his mother in a booby-trapped warehouse. The Joker's ultimate revenge would be driving his Dark Knight nemesis to the edge of madness with grief.

HARLEY QUINN
Dr. Harleen Quinzel fell head over heels for the Joker during a brief internship at Arkham Asylum. While there she aided his frequent escapes and earned her own padded cell. To win the love of her "Puddin'," Quinzel liberated herself and pursued him in the ultimate "love/hate" relationship as the curvaceous jester Harley Quinn!

"PERHAPS YOU'LL KILL ME..."

ACID TOUCH
With a preference for chemical weapons, the Joker wields corrosive acids and "Joker Venom," a binary compound which poisons his victims in laughing spasms, their death masks mirroring his own ruby-red leer.

PSYCHO-KILLER
Plotting high-concept heists one day and random violence the next, the Joker's motives follow no predictable pattern. He is just as likely to reward loyal henchmen as he is to shoot them for laughing out of turn. Even the estranged Harley Quinn finds her ex-boyfriend emotionally erratic and undeniably unsafe!

CATWOMAN

LIKE ALL CATS, *femme fatale* Selina Kyle always manages to land on her feet. Yet another orphan of Gotham City's mean streets, a young and destitute Selina escaped an abusive state home to live by her wits and petty theft, vowing never to want for anything again. In a backstreet dojo, Selina sharpened her claws and mastered ninja arts as basic job skills in cat burglary. As "Catwoman," she lined her purse in a long string of daring heists, eluding capture by the Dark Knight… but not escaping his notice. More altruistic than she would ever admit, Selina occasionally plies her larcenous trade in order to help Gotham's fellow "castaways." A bright, shiny bauble, however, can still catch this thief's sultry green eyes.

DRAMATIC PAWS
Make no mistake, this kitten has claws… and she isn't afraid to use them! Though not a formal martial arts stylist, Selina practices a smattering of several disciplines, including Jeet Kune Do and Jujitsu, as well as a few boxing moves taught to her by ex-heavyweight champ Ted Grant, once the hard-hitting hero Wildcat!

WHIP SMART
Catwoman wields an 8-ft braided leather bullwhip, as well as a steel-bearing-tipped cat-o'-nine-tails, both useful as weapons or acrobatic accouterments.

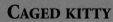

SSWWW. THCK

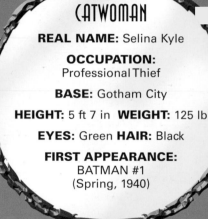

CATWOMAN

REAL NAME: Selina Kyle

OCCUPATION: Professional Thief

BASE: Gotham City

HEIGHT: 5 ft 7 in **WEIGHT:** 125 lb

EYES: Green **HAIR:** Black

FIRST APPEARANCE: BATMAN #1 (Spring, 1940)

CAGED KITTY

Catwoman became the first costumed criminal to test the G.C.P.D.'s "zero tolerance" policy for wrongdoing in post-NML Gotham. Captured and unmasked by the police, Selina refused to divulge her true identity and was sentenced as "Jane Doe" to the Cinque Center, a women's reformatory which dredged up all her childhood fears of being caged. Fellow inmate Harley Quinn played upon these memories and duped Catwoman into a revenge scheme against Commissioner James Gordon, placing the escaped Selina at further odds with the law!

GREEN-EYED LADY
Selina Kyle has hobnobbed with Gotham's elite to pick their pockets, but otherwise remains a raven-haired mystery. She maintains her anonymity with a string of aliases and always pays her debts in cash.

ARCTIC STEALTH
Depending on the caper, Catwoman's wardrobe provides a cat-costume for practically any need. During Gotham's Ebola Gulf-A plague outbreak, she donned an insulated and camouflaged "Snow-Cat" suit, aiding the Bat-Family by trekking through the Canadian Yukon to track down a cure.

Bullwhip

Form-fitting spandex

THE FELINE FORM
Catwoman's costume is designed for freedom of movement, but is neither fire-retardant nor bullet-resistant. However, Starlite lenses in her cowl enhance Catwoman's night-vision, while retractable claws in both gloves and boots assist climbing and are sharp enough to shred body armor.

Leather glove

THE CAT AND THE BAT
Though she would deny her attraction for Batman is anything more than a kittenish flirtation, Catwoman is drawn to the Dark Knight on many levels, finding his valiant and incorruptible altruism as priceless as any gem.

TRAPPED BY BAST
To catch a thief, the G.C.P.D. enticed Catwoman with a rare Egyptian artifact, a statuette of the cat-goddess Bast. As the police cut off her every escape, Selina realized that Bast had betrayed her – inside the idol was a tiny tracking device!

Two-Face

TWO-FACE

REAL NAME: Harvey Dent

OCCUPATION: Professional Criminal

BASE: Gotham City

HEIGHT: 6 ft **WEIGHT:** 182 lb

EYES: Blue **HAIR:** Brown/Gray

FIRST APPEARANCE: DETECTIVE COMICS #66 (August, 1942)

"APOLLO" DENT
As handsome as he was brilliant, Harvey Dent was dubbed "Apollo" by a Gotham media enamored with the young, crusading district attorney.

HARVEY DENT is a man divided. Childhood abuse fractured Dent's psyche right down the middle, leaving respected Gotham District Attorney Harvey Dent subconsciously sublimating a darker and more violent persona as an adult. Fittingly, this duality was mirrored in Dent's good-luck charm, a "two-headed" silver dollar. Once Batman's ally in justice, Dent's evil side reared its ugly head when, amid a packed courtroom, gangster Vincent Maroni hurled acid in the D.A.'s handsome visage. As the left side of Dent's face dissolved, so did the psychic walls keeping his dark reflection in check. With good and evil wrestling for control, Dent scarred his lucky piece so that it would be the final arbiter for his new persona, Two-Face, a schizoid criminal mastermind, whose every vile act would be decided by the flip of a coin!

DAMAGING TESTIMONY
Facing an airtight case against him, crime boss Vincent Maroni refused to go down without evening the score against Dent. Maroni threw acid – smuggled to him by Assistant D.A. Adrian Fields – in Dent's face and was shot dead by court bailiffs!

DOUBLE JEOPARDY

Without Dr. Rudolph Klemper, Two-Face might not exist! Apprehended by Batman, Klemper had savagely murdered 16 elderly Gothamites. But prosecutor Harvey Dent lacked sufficient evidence to convict the serial killer, who was acquitted of all charges. Knowing he could not be re-tried for his crimes, Klemper – who admitted to multiple personalities – gleefully confessed his sins to Dent, whom he believed to be a kindred schizophrenic spirit. Klemper was too correct in his diagnosis, perishing shortly thereafter from a bomb planted by Dent's emerging dark half.

IN SICKNESS AND IN HEALTH
Despite Harvey's horrific injury, Gilda Grace Dent trusted that facial reconstruction would mend her husband's ghastly profile. But Harvey's scars were more than skin deep, and Gilda divorced Harvey after numerous plastic surgeries and years of psychiatric care failed to eclipse Two-Face's evil.

KILL ALL THE LAWYERS
Believing that justice is arbitrary, Harvey Dent holds any practitioner of the law in great contempt. As judge, jury, and executioner, Two-Face has murdered his own court-appointed attorneys and carried out lethal litigation against scores of Gotham legal eagles.

....ACQUITTED.... ...IT'S MY FAULT.

HEADS YOU WIN...
Sometimes the good side prevails. Never one to turn down an even bet, Two-Face let his lucky silver dollar decide the fate of a dying Batman, poisoned by himself, the Joker, and the Penguin. When Robin offered a coin-toss for the antidote, Dent lost the flip and strong-armed the Penguin to relinquish the cure!

JUSTICE DIVIDED
Dent returned to prosecution during No Man's Land, indicting Jim Gordon for his law-breaking alliance with Two-Face. But Dent's own cross-examination of his alter-ego led to Gordon's acquittal, much to Two-Face's addled disappointment.

TWO SIDES OF LOVE
A prisoner of Two-Face for five long months during NML, Renee Montoya glimpsed a kinder and gentler Harvey Dent, one who loved the G.C.P.D. detective enough to send flowers on her twenty-eighth birthday.

THE PENGUIN

LITTLE OZZIE
Squat and stout as a boy, Oswald was easy prey for school bullies who dubbed him "Penguin."

OSWALD CHESTERFIELD COBBLEPOT is a rare bird among the Batman's foes: he has actually made crime pay! Nattily attired in top hat and tails, Cobblepot is better known as "The Penguin," a criminal mastermind with a penchant for ornithology and trick umbrellas concealing automatic weapons, flame-throwers – or *worse*. Tiring of the Dark Knight foiling his every scheme, Cobblepot abandoned his parasols and opened Gotham's most famous nightclub, The Iceberg Lounge. Behind this less-than-legitimate business front, the Penguin continues his larcenous ways as a "fixer" entrenched in the Gotham underworld and one step removed from Batman's reach.

BIRDS OF A FEATHER

Cobblepot's fascination with ornithology dates back to his early childhood when his widowed mother ran a pet shop specializing in exotic birds. Short, paunchy, and burdened with a prominent, aquiline nose, Oswald's school-yard nickname, "Penguin," was made worse by his mother's vehemence that he carry an umbrella, even on cloudless days. Mrs. Cobblepot feared that her son might succumb to pneumonia – just as his father had – after a sudden, sharp, cold rain shower. Oswald's spirits were comforted by his feathered friends in the pet shop. These birds became his constant companions in the years that followed, when the Penguin turned to crime in order to acquire the wealth and power necessary to rise above all those who ridiculed him.

Top hat often conceals small arms

Tempered steel sword-blade

Monocle laser-lens

CORPORATE TAKEOVER
The Penguin recently weathered an attempt to close down his celebrated Iceberg Lounge nightclub when Bruce Wayne purchased the building and became his new landlord! Rather than evict his unsavory tenant, Wayne has allowed Cobblepot to remain, keeping the black marketeer right where the Dark Knight can watch over him.

Concealed .22 revolver in ankle holster

FOWL PLAY
Agile despite his rotundity, the Penguin is an able fighter. His trained avian accomplices have included jackdaws, eagles, and nightingales.

PENGUIN

REAL NAME: Oswald Chesterfield Cobblepot

OCCUPATION: Restaurateur/Racketeer

BASE: Gotham City

HEIGHT: 5 ft 2 in **WEIGHT:** 175 lb

EYES: Blue **HAIR:** Black

FIRST APPEARANCE: DETECTIVE COMICS #58 (December, 1941)

SPRING-LOADED
The Penguin's "Pogo-rella" employed a high-tensile titanium-coiled spring, capable of vaulting him considerable heights and distances for fast getaways.

PENGUIN FLIGHT
In addition to rocket-propelled one-man parasols, the Penguin has also adapted umbrella canopies to serve as parachutes or spinning helicopter rotors.

ADVANCE WARNING
A rear-view mirror on his umbrella-handle warns the Penguin of sneak-attacks, giving him time to fire bullets, poison darts, or even the germs of *psittacosis*, the pneumonia-like "Parrot Fever"!

Trained carrier pigeon

BREAD AND CIRCUSES
During NML, the Penguin was perhaps the most powerful man in Gotham, dominating the commerce of what little food or valuables remained. He offered servitude in exchange for a piece of overripe fruit or a can of beans. The Penguin's avarice was further demonstrated in the toppled Davenport Towers, where the entertainment included the bartering of human lives in deadly gladiatorial games!

Retractable blade in wing-tip shoe

NOLAN

THE RIDDLER

MASTER PLANNER
Edward Nigma delights in his cunning creativity.

CONUNDRUMS are the mania of Edward Nigma. Suffering an obsessive-compulsive desire for attention, Nigma's disorder unfortunately manifests itself in malfeasance. As the Riddler, he has attempted to steal the spotlight from Gotham City's other notable career criminals by concocting the most cryptic crimes, each prefaced by clues in the form of inscrutable riddles. Though utterly perplexing to Gotham's Finest, Nigma's puzzles find a formidable opponent in the Batman, whose deductive skills have proven superior to the Riddler's enigmatic engineering. Incarcerated more often than not, Nigma wracks his brain to plot that one mystery the Dark Knight *won't* be able to solve.

ANSWERS TO EVERY QUESTION

In psychological interviews, Edward Nigma admits that his quest to rise above anonymity has roots in his youth. In a school contest, Nigma (then Eddie Nashton) cheated in order to assemble a puzzle more quickly than his classmates. With the prize came respect, recognition, and the notice of bullies who rarely appreciated Eddie's "cleverness." As an adult, Edward would have demonstrated his mental superiority to Gotham's police if not for a bullying Batman. Though he claims that his crimes are "performance art," Nigma's misdeeds mask a deeper yearning – to be loved!

SLEIGHT-OF-HAND
An admirer of late great escape artist Harry Houdini, the Riddler's tangled trap displays a similar flair for dramatic showmanship.

THE RIDDLER

REAL NAME: Eddie Nashton (aka Edward Nigma)

OCCUPATION: Professional Criminal

BASE: Gotham City

HEIGHT: 6 ft 1 in **WEIGHT:** 183 lb

EYES: Blue **HAIR:** Black

FIRST APPEARANCE: DETECTIVE COMICS #140 (October, 1948)

AARGH!

SHOCK ATTACK!
Though years of beatings have increased Nigma's tolerance for pain, he's more apt to pick up a weapon – like this stun-gun – than engage in fisticuffs.

PUZZLE OR DIE!
Nigma thought his greatest death-trap was inescapable! In a true no-win scenario, the Riddler coralled Batman in a flooding room with walls of live-wires. To remain meant drowning, while scaling the walls meant certain electrocution. Yet Batman still figured a way out of the trap.

CRAZY TALK
Safe in the padded cells of Arkham Asylum, Nigma ponders the unsolvable riddle of his own psychosis.

Echo

Query

GIRL POWER
The Riddler's gang of two are blonde Diedre Vance and brunette Nina Damfino – aka Query and Echo, respectively – violent femmes with a knack for finishing each other's sentences.

Poison Ivy

CHLOROPHYLL, not blood, courses through the veins of Pamela Isley. Transformed by the self-styled "Floronic Man," Jason Woodrue, the shrinking violet Isley bloomed into the ravishing Poison Ivy, a human/plant hybrid whose skin was toxic to the touch and shed fragrant pheromones capable of entangling men in her charms. Ivy used these abilities for thievery, thus becoming a thorn in Batman's side. But as her human side withered, Ivy grew more passionately intolerant of abuses against Nature's flora, making herself over as a self-styled guerrilla guardian of the green. She nurtured Gotham's polluted Robinson Park into a verdant haven for the wayward orphans of No Man's Land, relinquishing control only to spare the park's defoliation. Ivy nevertheless has more seeds to sow.

HOPE SPRINGS ETERNAL

Ivy's willingness to provide food and shelter to the children of disaster may signal a more permanent shift towards altruism on her part. In addition to the human "sprouts" she nurtured during NML, Ivy also cared for an injured Harley Quinn. Only time will tell if their blossoming friendship means more to Ivy's personal growth than just a comely criminal collaboration.

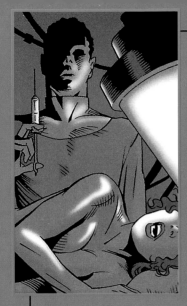

WEIRD SCIENCE
Though he lured her with words of love, Dr. Woodrue's interest in Pamela Isley was purely scientific.

BAD MUSHROOMS
When Ivy first set down roots in Gotham, she greeted the city with a deadly fleshy fungi of the class *Basidiomycetes*. Threatening to scatter her fast-growing mushroom spores in Gotham's water supply, Ivy demanded $10,000,000 as ransom for the smothering toadstools' antidote!

POISON IVY

REAL NAME:
Pamela Lillian Isley

OCCUPATION:
Professional Criminal

BASE: Gotham City

HEIGHT: 5 ft 6 in **WEIGHT:** 110 lb

EYES: Green **HAIR:** Chestnut

FIRST APPEARANCE:
BATMAN #181
(June, 1966)

KISS ME DEADLY

After Woodrue's torturous botanical experiments, the timid Isley blossomed into a real man-killer, eager to attract and dominate men with her poison kiss. Like her namesake, *Rhus radicans*, Ivy excretes the blistering sap Urushiol, a narcotic or necrotic depending on her whim.

IVY VERSUS CLAYFACE

In the winter of NML, Poison Ivy was taken captive by cruel and lustful Basil Karlo, the Ultimate Clayface. Denied water and sunlight, the weakened Ivy watched helplessly as Clayface forced her gang of children to harvest the Park's fruits and vegetables as high-priced produce for a starving Gotham. With Batman's aid, Ivy escaped to take revenge upon Karlo, using his rich clay body as compost to fertilize her plants!

Genetically modified tiger lily

POISONING THE PARK

Pressured by Mayor Dickerson to evict Poison Ivy, the G.C.P.D. Quick Response Team prepared to liquefy the vegetation of Robinson Park with the military herbicide RC-60. Though resolved to martyr herself for the park, Ivy relented, realizing that she cared for her endangered orphan charges as much as her beloved flora.

FATAL FOLIAGE

Ivy's body is a witches' brew of allergens, manifesting both the toxins and antitoxins for Rattlepod, Nightshade, Flixweed, and other deadly greens. Ivy also wields genetically-mutated seed pods which germinate into swiftly growing strangling lianas, stabbing cacti, and other menaces!

HERE COME THE FERAKS!

Ivy guarded Robinson Park with thorny "Feraks," a wild mix of human and plant DNA.

MR. FREEZE

FROZEN FRIENDS
To escape the pressures of his brutal father, young Victor Fries developed an unusual hobby: freezing animals! Victor believed he was preserving his pretty pets forever; his therapist thought Victor was trying to control his own unpredictable world.

COLD-HEARTED is merely the tip of the iceberg in describing Victor Fries. His body chemistry altered to frigidity by a hail of super-coolants, the brilliant cryogenicist must forever wear a suit of air-conditioned armor to remain comfortably chilled. Wielding an ice-blasting cold gun, Mr. Freeze revenged himself upon Gothcorp, the soulless corporation that denied him funding to continue the research necessary to save his beloved wife Nora. Victor had placed her in suspended animation to halt the rare malady consuming her. But an ensuing clash with the Batman shattered any hope for Nora's recovery. Accidentally firing his cold gun at Nora's cryo-chamber, Freeze fractured her slumbering body into a million dead shards. This act he blames upon the Dark Knight with the fury of a raging blizzard.

Liquid super-coolant

THE LOVE OF HIS LIFE
Isolated and ridiculed at boarding school and college, Fries believed he would never enjoy the warm touch of humanity. Then came Nora, the beautiful athlete who stole his heart.

MR. FREEZE
REAL NAME: Dr. Victor Fries
OCCUPATION: Professional Criminal
BASE: Gotham City
HEIGHT: 6 ft **WEIGHT:** 190 lb
EYES: Blue **HAIR:** None
FIRST APPEARANCE: BATMAN #121 (February, 1959)

COLD SHOWER
When Nora was stricken, Victor left a teaching post to work for Gothcorp. There he specialized in cryogenics, hoping to prolong Nora's life until a cure could be found. Gothcorp's decision to pull the plug on Nora's cryo-chamber resulted in a stand-off, which ended with Victor falling into his own experimental coolants!

90

Shatterproof acrylic bubble

SHATTERED HEARTS

One by one, Freeze eliminated Gothcorp's executives on a mission to destroy CEO Ferris Boyle. Though Batman offered aid for Nora's plight, Freeze was so blinded by his vendetta that he inadvertently blasted her cryo-chamber! And so died the last embers of his humanity.

AGHHH...!

FROZEN ASSETS

The super-cooled laser matrices of Freeze's gun and armor are fueled by a different sort of "ice," only the largest and most perfect diamonds. Without such gems, Freeze requires refrigeration units in order to escape his suit. Otherwise, his skin would broil and his lungs would melt!

CHILLED TO THE BONE

Determined to have his revenge upon the Dark Knight, Freeze flash-froze Robin! As the young hero's vital signs plummeted, Batman captured Freeze and reverse-engineered the frigid foe's cold gun in order to thaw Tim Drake's icy tomb!

Armor composed of pliant, thermally-stable plastics

RĀ'S AL GHŪL

TALIA
Talia's fierce loyalty to her father is tested by her passion for the Dark Knight. She would willingly die for either man, but refuses to be a pawn in their ongoing battles.

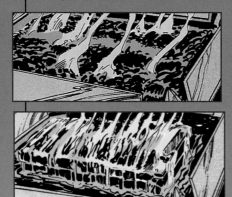

LAZARUS PITS
For Rā's al Ghūl, life eternal entails periodic immersion in Lazarus Pits excavated above the electromagnetic ley lines crisscrossing the Earth. Once filled with an alchemical brew of exotic poisons, the Pits are charged with the power to heal injuries and suspend aging.

To SAVE THE PLANET, he would destroy every last living soul. For untold centuries, Rā's al Ghūl has cheated death with alchemical "Lazarus Pits" extending his longevity to nigh-immortality so that he might restore Earth's ecological harmony. To achieve this Eden, Rā's al Ghūl commands an army of zealously devoted followers – chief among them his mortal daughter Talia – eco-terrorists willing to commit genocide on a global scale in the name of "The Demon's Head." Standing in opposition to this dystopian world order is the Batman, ironically the one man Rā's al Ghūl considers worthy enough to win Talia's hand in marriage and inherit Paradise.

APOCALYPSE NOW!

With the dawn of the new millennium, Rā's al Ghūl has increased his assault upon humankind with an even greater fervor. Unfortunately, Gotham City has been a focal point for the fulfillment of this apocalyptic agenda. The Demon's Head created the Ebola Gulf-A strain – dubbed "The Clench" – which killed thousands of Gotham's citizens. Rā's al Ghūl considered the outbreak merely a prelude to a panoply of virulence he would unleash upon the world, once he had deciphered the "Wheel of Plagues," an ancient mechanism that unlocked the genetic codes of terrible diseases. But Batman and his allies forestalled humanity's end, destroyed the Wheel, and denied Rā's al Ghūl his cruel legacy of extinction.

Rā's is a cunning swordsman and master of innumerable killing arts

WAKING THE DEAD
Immortality is not without its risks. A side effect of the life-prolonging process is a temporary raging madness that seizes Rā's al Ghūl upon his emergence from the Lazarus Pit. For this reason, he is left entirely alone following the rejuvenation, until his sanity returns.

RĀ'S AL GHŪL*

REAL NAME: Unknown
(*Translated: "The Demon's Head")

OCCUPATION: International Terrorist

BASE: Mobile

HEIGHT: 6 ft 5 in **WEIGHT:** 215 lb

EYES: Green **HAIR:** Gray with white streaks

FIRST APPEARANCE:
BATMAN #232
(June, 1971)

EXPERIENCE IS POWER
Though he has lost love and his own true name to the sands of time, Rā's al Ghūl has amassed other riches to fill the treasuries of his nomadic kingdom. But his greatest wealth is knowledge, both sacred and profane, culled during his long wanderings.

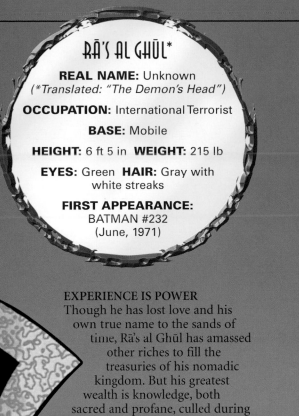

WHISPER A'DAIRE AND KYLE ABBOT
Agents loyal to Rā's al Ghūl, the serpentine Whisper A'Daire and man-wolf Kyle Abbot peddled immortality to Gotham in the form of a highly-addictive genetics-altering elixir.

UBU
Rā's al Ghūl's most loyal servant and protector – chosen through mortal combat – is called "Ubu," an honor once bestowed upon Bane when the Demon's Head briefly considered him as a potential mate for Talia.

BANE

OSOITO

As a child convict, Bane endured unthinkable cruelties. His only solace was a teddy bear, Osoito, a gift from one of the few Catholic missionaries permitted entrance to Pena Duro.

EXPERIMENTS IN PAIN

The Santa Priscan military hoped Venom would provide a battalion of unstoppable soldiers. Previous test subjects had died horribly, but Bane alone survived the surgical implants that pumped the drug directly into his cerebral cortex!

PUMPING UP

Bane injected measured doses of Venom into his cortico-implants via controls on his wrist-gauntlet.

HE IS BANE. He knows no other name. Born into captivity, the child who would become Bane was fated to fulfill his father's life sentence inside the wretched walls of Santa Prisca's Pena Duro prison fortress. Survival for Bane resided in meditation and smuggled books, which his starving mind devoured as his body grew strong on the rats trapped with him in the dreaded Cavidad Obscuro, a dank solitary cell below sea-level. Freedom lay in "Venom," an experimental steroid that granted the already formidable Bane the raging strength necessary to liberate himself from Pena Duro. Victory, however, could only be found in Gotham City, where Bane would gain infamy as the man who succeeded above all others in breaking the Bat!

KNIGHTFALL

Bane accomplished what other villains could not: he defeated the Dark Knight. Having studied the stratagems of military conquerors throughout history, Bane knew a direct assault was futile. So he did just the opposite, destroying Arkham Asylum and unleashing an army of maniacal villains to wear Batman down first. When the Dark Knight's stamina was spent, Bane attacked him in Wayne Manor, having deduced the hero's true identity. As their epic battle tumbled into the Batcave below, the cavern echoed with the resounding crack of Batman's shattering spine!

LexCorp tri-barrel .223-round chaingun

CROC WRESTLING!

Even with broken arms bound in plaster casts, Killer Croc contested Bane's underworld takeover. In the sewers beneath Gotham, Bane proved his supremacy!

FELONIOUS FRIENDS
Bane escaped Pena Duro with three loyal comrades in tow: the Neanderthal-like Trogg, the pale knife-wielding Zombie, and the skilled falconer known simply as Bird.

WHO RULES THE NIGHT?

Bane's dominion over Gotham was short-lived. As Bruce Wayne battled his crippling injuries, Jean Paul Valley assumed the mantle of the Dark Knight and violently took back the city. Eventually, the replacement Batman faced Bane, defeating the artificial strength of Venom with "The System" of St. Dumas. Bane later rid himself of his addiction to Venom, rebuilding his formidable physique muscle by muscle.

Peregrine falcon trained to gouge eyes with its talons

KRAKT

BANE

REAL NAME: Unknown

OCCUPATION: Professional Criminal

BASE: International

HEIGHT: 6 ft 8 in **WEIGHT:** 350 lb

EYES: Brown **HAIR:** Brown

FIRST APPEARANCE:
BATMAN:
VENGEANCE OF BANE
#1 (January, 1993)

SCARECROW

BE AFRAID!
Scarecrow practices the "Crane style" of violent dance.

AWKWARD AND GANGLY as a youth, Jonathan Crane overcame the school yard bullies who called him "Scarecrow" by conquering his own fears and delving into the study of dread. A professor of psychology and biochemistry in adulthood, he revenged himself on the Gotham University regents who fired him for his unorthodox teaching methods by quite literally scaring them to their deaths. As the Scarecrow, Crane used fright as a weapon, creating personalized phobias with his diabolical "fear gas" in order to further his criminal reign of terror.

HROORA
HROO

HEY, HE'S A
SCARECROW!

ANXIETIES OF YOUTH

Jonathan Crane endured the taunts of his fellow schoolchildren, who likened the youth – with his herky-jerky gait – both to a cornfield Scarecrow and the spindly, bookish Ichabod Crane of Washington Irving's *The Legend of Sleepy Hollow*.

THE TASTE OF FEAR
Crane immersed himself in the biochemical analysis of fear during his years at Gotham University. In time, he would synthesize terror into his own potent potable, a hallucinatory fear gas capable of creating waking nightmares!

SCARECROW

REAL NAME:
Prof. Jonathan Crane

OCCUPATION:
Professional Criminal

BASE: Gotham City

HEIGHT: 6 ft **WEIGHT:** 140 lb

EYES: Blue **HAIR:** Brown

FIRST APPEARANCE:
WORLD'S FINEST COMICS
#3 (Fall, 1941)

Scarecrow's costume of loose and ragged tatters is designed to strike fear and enable limber movement

THE ESSENCE OF FEAR

The Scarecrow's fear gas is a toxic mix of synthetic adreno-cortical secretions and strong hallucinogens. Released from a customized, skull-shaped atomizer, the fear gas prompts neuromuscular spasms, cardiac arrhythmia, and panic attacks as it augments a victim's personal phobias to terrifying levels.

NIGHT TERRORS

The Scarecrow's initial battle with Gotham's Dark Knight culminated in the acquisition of a new paralyzing horror all his own: *Chiropteraphobia,* an all-consuming fear of bats!

SCARE TACTICS

Schoolmates Bo Griggs and Sherry Squires paid the ultimate price for belittling Jonathan Crane after meeting his vengeful alter-ego, the Scarecrow!

DANGEROUS MINDS

The Scarecrow finds madness to the left of him and maniacal laughter to the right as yet another infamous patient of Arkham Asylum.

97

MAN-BAT

GENETIC PANACEA
Kirk hoped his animal genome research would reveal cures for all human ailments, including his own deafness. When his benefactors denied further funding, Kirk experimented on himself!

Man-Bat's wingspan averages 13 ft 5 in

NOBODY UNDERSTANDS BATS like zoologist Kirk Langstrom, for it takes one to know one! A renowned authority on the winged order *Chiroptera*, Langstrom labored to isolate and synthesize the chemical stimuli that fuel these creatures' unique echo-location abilities. His bat-gland extract did that and more, mutating Langstrom into a crazed half-human/half-bat monstrosity when he foolishly tested the serum on himself. Only through the intervention of his fiancée Francine and Gotham's *other* "Batman" would Langstrom regain his humanity. Though Kirk later refined the extract and aided the Dark Knight as an occasional crime-fighting comrade, his animal side would eventually dominate, making "Man-Bat" both a blessing and a curse to Kirk, Francine, and the burgeoning Langstrom family.

LAB PARTNER
Kirk's true love, Dr. Francine Lee, helped to synthesize the anti-serum which restored his human form.

MAN-BAT FAMILY

Though still wrestling with his Man-Bat persona, which reappears occasionally when latent elements of the Bat-Extract bring about his physical transformation, Kirk has settled into a modicum of "normal life" with his family. Kirk, Francine, daughter Rebecca, and son Aaron have settled in a rural hamlet midway between Gotham and Blüdhaven, where the former Man-Bat now serves as Director of Genetics Study at STAR Haven Labs.

BAD MEDICINE
The bat-extract restored Kirk's hearing, though not without unwelcome side-effects. As his ears became hyper-sensitive, a horrified Kirk found his entire genetic structure transforming into a hideous human/bat hybrid.

A TRUE BAT-MAN
Subduing Man-Bat is no mean feat. Fully transformed, Kirk Langstrom possesses great strength and the ability to fly. Augmented hearing and a bat's natural sonar allow him to navigate even in pitch darkness.

MAN-BAT

REAL NAME: Dr. Robert Kirkland Langstrom

OCCUPATION: Zoologist

BASE: Gotham City

HEIGHT: 6 ft 1 in **WEIGHT:** 201 lb

EYES: (as Langstrom) Brown; (as Man-Bat) Red **HAIR:** Brown

FIRST APPEARANCE:
DETECTIVE COMICS #400
(June, 1970)

BAY-BEEEEE!

LIKE FATHER, LIKE SON

During No Man's Land, while Kirk went missing in a Man-Bat fugue, Francine and her daughter Becky transformed themselves with the Bat-Extract to protect "Baby-Bat" Aaron Langstrom from rogues eager to capitalize on his developing hyper-senses. Unlike his sister Becky, Aaron was born mutated because the Bat-Extract had altered Kirk's DNA. Unfortunately, Kirk passed these genes on to his son.

TURF WAR
Attracted by a swarm of bats returning home for their diurnal rest, Man-Bat inadvertently discovered the Batcave. He was soon involved in a territorial conflict with the cavern's true resident!

VENTRILOQUIST & SCARFACE

GALLOWS HUMOR
Facing life imprisonment, Donnegan entertained himself by carving the lightning-charred remains of the Gallows Tree into a wooden dummy. Ironically, "Woody" turned upon Donnegan, enlisting cell-mate Arnold Wesker to hang his creator!

QUAKEMASTER
The shock of Gotham's Cataclysm may have precipitated another of Wesker's personas, Quakemaster. Claiming responsibility for the devastation, Quakemaster demanded a $100,000,000 ransom or else he would unleash another "crustal displacement"!

Mini Thompson submachine gun

ARNOLD WESKER'S NO DUMMY, though his evil alter-ego Scarface most certainly is. Orphaned as a child, the timid Wesker repressed his feelings so deeply that he developed multiple personalities to cope with life's stresses. When Wesker finally loosed his pent-up emotions, he killed a man in a barroom brawl and was sentenced to Blackgate Penitentiary. There he first encountered the puppet Scarface, who had been whittled by an inmate named Donnegan from the wood of Blackgate's Gallows Tree. Wesker murdered Scarface's maker and gave the gruesome gangster doll a voice. Together, Scarface and the allegedly "unwilling" Ventriloquist carved out a significant niche in Gotham's underworld. It remains unclear who's really pulling the strings in their bizarre relationship.

THROWING THEIR VOICES

Pleading himself an accessory to Scarface's crimes, Wesker has successfully convinced Gotham's courts that his sanity is in question, necessitating treatment in Arkham Asylum. Dr. Jeremiah Arkham's psychological profile finds that Wesker's anti-social personality uses the Scarface dummy as a conduit to commit violent crimes. Wesker himself believes that Scarface is haunted by the souls of the 313 men hanged upon the Gallows Tree from which the dummy was sculpted. One thing is certain: Evil follows Scarface wherever he goes, whether or not it is ingrained in the very wood.

SOCKO!
When Bane freed Arkham's patients to belabor and exhaust Batman, Ventriloquist was minus his partner-in-crime. Thus, the evil "Socko" was born, later vying for supremacy with the returned Scarface. The two solved their differences in a shoot-out, leaving Wesker with bullet-riddled hands.

HEAD TRAUMA
After Quakemaster was revealed as just another of Wesker's puppets, the Ventriloquist took up Scarface once more and fled in a hail of bullets. Gotham Police Lt. Mackenzie Bock knew the only way to stop Wesker was to silence Scarface, shattering his wooden head with a single shot!

Wide-brimmed fedora conceals pearl-handled Derringer

Hinged jaw

THREE'S A CROWD
Convinced by Dr. Arkham to rid himself of Scarface forever, Wesker reluctantly complied. But as the Ventriloquist found legitimate fame with the pretty puppet Lola, a jealous Scarface waited in the wings…

Hand-sewn silk tie

Puppet strings woven from prison-issue dental floss

HE'S THE GOSS!
Though able to manipulate Scarface with either hand, the Ventriloquist's skills do not extend to pronouncing the letter "B." When shouting defiance at the Dynamic Duo, Scarface calls them "Gatman and Rogin."

VENTRILOQUIST

REAL NAME: Arnold Wesker

OCCUPATION: Professional Criminal

BASE: Gotham City

HEIGHT: 5 ft 7 in **WEIGHT:** 142 lb

EYES: Blue **HAIR:** Gray

FIRST APPEARANCE:
DETECTIVE COMICS #583
(February, 1988)

CHARAXES

DRURY WALKER was little more than a joke.
As Killer Moth, he offered his services as paid protector to
Gotham's gangsters. But despite an arsenal of ingenious
weaponry, including his signature cocoon gun, the colorful
Killer Moth was bested by Batman at every turn,
leaving his clients both irate *and* incarcerated.
Then Batgirl defeated the Moth, earning Walker further
ridicule. So he made a deal with a devil – the tempter
Neron – who gave Walker his heart's desire.
What Walker wanted most was to be feared.
But what he received in exchange for his soul
was metamorphosis into a real Killer
Moth… the man-eating Charaxes!

*Even in his dreams,
Killer Moth was
a failure...*

CHARAXES

REAL NAME: Drury Walker
(aka Cameron Van Cleer)

BASE: Gotham City

HEIGHT: 6 ft 9 in **WINGSPAN:** 12 ft

WEIGHT: 202 lb **EYES:** Red

HAIR: Mustard Yellow

FIRST APPEARANCE:
UNDERWORLD UNLEASHED
#1 (November, 1995)

*…but as Charaxes,
the Moth evolved
into the stuff of
nightmares!*

SOUL PROVIDER

Like a host of other power-hungry
villains, Drury Walker eagerly
responded to Neron's offer, enduring
hellish pain as the demon lord
fulfilled his pitiful wish. From
Walker's transforming cocoon, the
frightful Charaxes emerged to feast
upon his keepers at Arkham!

15091

LEFTOVERS
A rare carnivore among *Lepidoptera*, Charaxes prefers the juices of live prey to floral nectars. Spinning fibrous cocoons around his victims, Charaxes savors their fluids through piercing proboscises!

No longer human, Charaxes is driven by an insatiable appetite!

Robin struggles to escape a sticky chrysalis!

PEST CONTROL
Though his exoskeleton is not impervious to bullets, Charaxes shrugs off most firepower with ease. In his new insectoid form, Walker's strength is increased tenfold. Sharp prehensile feelers increase his deadly reach, while chitinous fore-wings and hind-wings powered by taut muscles in his thorax give Charaxes fluttering flight!

Lady Shiva

IN THE HINDU PANTHEON, Shiva is the "Destroyer of Worlds." With uncompromising hubris, Sandra Woosan has adopted this name as her own. Vengeance for her sister's murder first led Shiva to the martial arts; but more selfish ambitions spurred her to viciously ascend the League of Assassins' hierarchy over the battered bodies of countless opponents. A study in contradictions, she is credited with training Tim Drake to wield his Bo staff, as well as helping Bruce Wayne regain his fighting spirit after Bane broke his back. But as the "Paper Monkey" – ranking warrior in the clandestine Cult of the Monkey Fist – Shiva has also faced the Dark Knight and his squires in mortal combat. They trust Shiva only as far as they can throw her.

MARTIAL LAW

To hasten Bruce Wayne's return after he was injured by Bane, Shiva killed an armless sensei while wearing the mask of Tengu, a bat spirit. She passed the totem to Bruce, who was soon faced with seven deadly martial artists seeking vengeance for their master's death.

BROTHERHOOD OF THE FIST

In the martial arts underground, the Cult of the Monkey Fist represents the pinnacle of fighting perfection, a hierarchical pyramid with Shiva standing alone at its top, having slain all rivals to her supremacy. Holding the much-vaunted title of Paper Monkey, Shiva welcomes any combatant foolhardy enough to covet her status.

Speech bubbles:

LADY SHIVA. WE MEET AGAIN.

YOU SEEMED TO HAVE WEATHERED YOUR CAPTIVITY WELL.

THER-ACKK

KUNG-FU FIGHTER

Formerly Sandra Woosan's ally in her hunt for her sister's killer, martial arts guru Richard Dragon briefly became a reluctant operative of the spy network G.O.O.D. with Shiva and Bronze Tiger. Dragon retired from adventuring to seek the path of peace, but has emerged from seclusion to impart his unique expertise to Oracle and the Huntress.

A FAMILY AFFAIR

Batman encountered Shiva in the Middle East during Jason Todd's search to discover the identity of his real mother. One of three possible candidates, Shiva divulged that she was not Jason's mother only after the Dark Knight had bested her in personal combat and injected the martial mistress with the truth serum Sodium Pentothal.

THE KILLER ELITE

Throughout her pursuit of fighting perfection, Shiva has employed herself as an assassin-for-hire, often fulfilling her contracts with a single strike, her merciless "Leopard Blow."

LADY SHIVA

REAL NAME: Sandra Woosan

OCCUPATION: Mercenary

BASE: Mobile

HEIGHT: 5 ft 8 in **WEIGHT:** 115 lb

EYES: Blue **HAIR:** Black

FIRST APPEARANCE:
RICHARD DRAGON, KUNG-FU FIGHTER #5
(January, 1976)

HARD KNOCKS

Shiva showed Batgirl the folly of attacking her, eluding every blow and breaking several of her bones. One sucker-punch and a flying kick later, Batgirl agreed to battle Shiva a year hence in exchange for a single fighting lesson.

MAD HATTER

HEAD GAMES
Tetch's oversized hat often conceals small weapons and mind-bending electronics circuitry.

JERVIS TETCH lives in another world, seen through the looking glass of Lewis Carroll's beloved children's book *Alice's Adventures in Wonderland*. Utterly convinced that he is "The Mad Hatter," Tetch forever scarred the image of Carroll's hectoring haberdasher by kidnapping and brainwashing young girls as "Alices" in a white-slavery ring. When his sordid "tea party" was foiled by the Dynamic Duo, Tetch was remanded to Arkham Asylum for treatment for his bizarre psychological fixation. To date, his rehabilitation has been unsuccessful, and the mercurial Mad Hatter continues to draw inspiration from the fictional Wonderland for any number of mind-controlling schemes.

CAPPED OFF!
Having learned from previous perilous encounters, Batman has shielded his cowl against the Mad Hatter's hypnotic thrall.

AVID COLLECTOR

While the Mad Hatter of Carroll's tale was merely a vendor of hats, Jervis Tetch has an insane desire for caps of all manner, shape, and size. This hobby – supplemented by thievery, extortion, and other baser crimes – has led him to covet jeweled crowns, priceless antique headdresses, and even the cowl of his most hated foe!

FREQUENCY MODULATION
The Mad Hatter has taken hypnosis to new levels. He utilizes microwave transceivers in hats, helmets, or headphones to manipulate alpha waves in the brains of his victims, making them inordinately prone to suggestion.

MAD HATTER

REAL NAME: Jervis Tetch

OCCUPATION: Professional Criminal

BASE: Gotham City

HEIGHT: 4 ft 8 in   **WEIGHT:** 149 lb

EYES: Blue   **HAIR:** Red

FIRST APPEARANCE: BATMAN #49 (November, 1948)

SECRET STASH
During No Man's Land, Tetch remained in Gotham in order to excavate his beloved cache of unique chapeaux, stored inside a steel vault buried under tons of rubble.

LATE FOR TEA

In order to cater to the despicable tastes of Generalissimo Singh Manh Lee, the Mad Hatter abducted a number of blonde teenage girls. He planned to tranquilize them with drugged tea for a one-way trip to the Republic of Rheelasia aboard the dictator's personal yacht!

Tetch lulled the guests at his tea party with soporific music broadcast over a pirated radio channel.

HOODWINKED!
To win the mask of the nefarious Narcosis, Tetch agreed to help him bring hallucinogenic "bliss" to quake-shaken Gotham with the release of volatile toxic gasses.

WRATH OF ROBIN
When the Mad Hatter kidnapped one of the Boy Wonder's own schoolmates, Robin flew solo, defeating Tetch and liberating all of the kidnapped "Alices" without the aid of the Dark Knight.

Monstrous Mutations

THE WELCOME SIGN to Gotham City could quite conceivably read: "Here be monsters." Apart from the Joker, Two-Face, and Charaxes, Gotham is home to an unusual mix of the grotesque and macabre, some scarred by their own evil intentions, others victims of cruel and capricious fate, and more still with origins beyond this mortal coil. Perhaps by fault of its own pervasive Gothic exterior, the Dark Knight's troubled protectorate finds itself a nexus for creatures trapped behind frightful masks which they are unable to shed.

FREAKS AND GEEKS

Arguably, Gotham's significant populace of "monsters" might be enabled by both a predilection to crime and the city's overwhelming technological base. With WayneTech, STAR Labs, LexCorp, and other think-tanks engaged in all manner of scientific study, Gotham contains a veritable Pandora's Box of potential mutagens. And though valuable on the open market to competing researchers, these "magic potions" – be they bat-extracts or the blood of Clayfaces – tempt human frailty with the promise of unbridled power.

GEARHEAD
Nathan Finch's hatred for Batman is as cold and mechanical as his steely cybernetic body. Once battling the Dark Knight above a frozen river, Finch was forced to replace his frostbitten limbs with prosthetics, later wiring himself into a roving spider-legged battle-tank. More machine than man now, Gearhead will do anything to terminate his hated foe.

FIREFLY
Fueled by burning avarice, Garfield Lynns graduated from petty crime to professional arson, kindling an incendiary urge to pyromania within him. As the Napalm-spewing Firefly, Lynns tragically fell victim to one of his latter-day blazes, an inferno which scarred his entire body.

ORCA
Dr. Grace Balin sacrificed her own humanity to spare the homeless outcasts seeking refuge along Gotham's depressed waterfront. Balin's study of killer whales yielded a formula for spinal cord regeneration which allowed the paralyzed marine biologist to swim freely as the vengeful giantess Orca!

KILLER CROC
Waylon Jones suffers a unique skin disease that hardens his epidermis into the appearance of green-tinged scales. In his misbegotten youth, Jones went from a succession of reform schools to carnival sideshows, where he found freakish fame wrestling alligators as "Killer Croc." More ambitious career goals led Croc to Gotham, where he brutally muscled his way into the city's criminal underbelly. Currently, Croc grapples with his reptilian side while under psychiatric care in Arkham Asylum.

ARRAKHAT
An evil djinn of Middle Eastern myth, Arrakhat was summoned by Quraci forces to assassinate Tim Drake's schoolmate Ali Ben Khadir, Emir of Dhabar. Once called forth, Arrakhat must claim three lives before returning to his "Well of Flames."

THE MUDPACK
The malleable Clayfaces are among Batman's most formidable foes. Actor-turned-murderer Basil Karlo, the first Clayface, wore a garish mask of horrific make-up in homage to his greatest role. Clayface II Matt Hagen could mold his flesh at will. Acromegalic Preston Payne was the most grotesque Clayface of all, dissolving men to protoplasm with the merest touch. Sondra Fuller continued the legacy as Lady Clay, mimicking the form and abilities of anyone or anything. Not to be upstaged, Basil Karlo usurped the surviving Clayfaces' powers to become the undisputed "Ultimate Clayface." Payne and Fuller, meanwhile, fell in love and sired Cassius, a new and deadly mudslinger.

Murdering Maniacs

LADY KILLER
Though they have battled as Batman and Lady Vic, respectively, neither Bruce Wayne nor Lady Elaine realize their connection outside of costumes or social circles.

WHO SAYS CRIME DOESN'T PAY? Having the highest violent crime rate on record, Gotham City claims the unenviable title, "murder capital of the free world." And with this distinction comes an economic niche eagerly and energetically filled by all manner of assassins, mercenaries, and guns-for-hire. Elements of both costumed rogues and organized crime – split among the Lucky Hand Triad, Escabedo Cartel, Odessa Mob, Sicilian Mafia, and Burnley Town Massive (BTM) – employ any number of gunsels, both amateur and professional. Meanwhile, neighboring Blüdhaven is developing its own cottage industry of hitmen hired specifically to rid the city of the vigilante Nightwing.

KNIGHT-SLAYERS

Though many commit homicide for profit, a sizable number of Gotham's murderous maniacs kill for the sheer thrill of it. Those most prolific, the serial and spree killers, are confined to the wretched bowels of Arkham Asylum. Worst of all are the death-dealers who target human casualties merely to draw the attention of the Dark Knight, their most-desired victim.

LADY VIC
Descended from an eminent lineage of British mercenaries, Lady Elaine Marsh-Morton is one of the killer elite retained by Roland Desmond to eliminate Nightwing. To the hero's credit, Lady Vic – Marsh-Morton's professional sobriquet – has been unsuccessful thus far. Her personal arsenal, heirlooms of her ancestors' colonial campaigns, include a Webley-Fosberry .45.5 revolver, Bundi and kris daggers, Zulu Knobkerry and Asegai spear, Kukhris, and Thugee strangling cloth.

MR. ZSASZ
Victor Zsasz is the most unrepentant of sociopaths, a serial killer whose body count is etched indelibly into his skin. Highly intelligent and deceptively cunning, Mr. Zsasz – as he is known among the cult of celebrity associated with prolific predators – is indiscriminate in choosing his prey. However, he does prefer a carving knife for the slaughter, leaving his victims in natural "life-like" positions and marking their deaths as gashed tallies on his own body. Zsasz would consider a slice for Batman the sharpest cut in his macabre ritual of murder and self-mutilation.

STEELJACKET

His true identity unknown, Steeljacket is a horrific product of genetic manipulation to create a human/bird hybrid. Lightweight, brittle, hollow bones forced the formerly high-flying raptor to don protective metal armor, hence his *nom de guerre*. Though his wings were amputated following injuries sustained in an aerial battle with Robin, Steeljacket's claws remain as sharp and deadly as ever.

BRUTALE

Frequently paired with fellow stone-killer Randy Hanrahan, aka the steroid-pumped Stallion, Guillermo Barrera would also enjoy collecting the considerable bounty on Nightwing. A refugee of Hasaragua's fallen Marxist regime, the former state interrogator now peddles his "surgical skills" on the world market as the assassin Brutale, currently in the employ of Blockbuster. As in his military days, Brutale favors scalpels, throwing knives, and other razor-keen blades.

10.5-in throwing knife

ECHO

Enlisted by Two-Face during his attempted takeover of NML Gotham, the assassin known as "Echo" was once an operative of the Soviet GRU (*Glavnoye Razvedyvatelnoye Upravlenie*). Lone survivor of the "Turing Project," an experiment in wet-ware bio-mechanical implants, Echo is able to mentally scan electronic data transmission. This ability extends to the human mind's bio-electrical functions, allowing Echo to "read" thoughts – creating a constant and excruciating buzzing in her own troubled head.

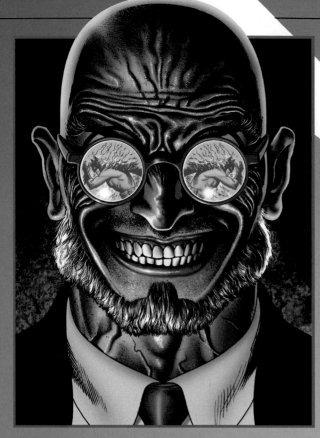

PROFESSOR HUGO STRANGE

As consultant to Gotham's "Vigilante Task Force," psychiatrist Hugo Strange's obsession with the mental dissection of the Dark Knight led to personal identification with his quarry. To prove his intellectual superiority, Strange sought to shatter Batman's mind, a battle of wills complicated after the Professor deduced Batman's true identity, knowledge he jealously guards as his own secret weapon!

MASTERMINDS

KNOWLEDGE CAN BE a dangerous thing, especially when wielded by criminal masterminds who skirt the very edges of sanity in their lust for power. Worse yet are the foes whose capacity for evil is overshadowed only by their insane intellects, some as keen as the Dark Knight's own. One genius foe attacks Batman on a psychological battlefield. Another has devised potent narcotic allures to seduce him. A third is perhaps even more at home in darkness than the Dark Knight or his squires. And the remaining venal virtuosos reign over dutiful foot-soldiers inspired to commit appalling crimes in their names!

MURDEROUS MINIONS

While some villains ply henchmen with the promise of wealth, the masterminds of Batman's Rogues Gallery ensure loyalty by other means. Hugo Strange turns men to monsters with mind and body-altering drugs. Nocturna bewitches with her own patented perfumes. Maxie Zeus rules over mortals convinced by his claim to godhood, while Black Mask instills his fellow False-Facers with the belief that they are similarly empowered by their own masks. General McGog dominates his well-trained regiments with fear, punishing insubordination with death, while King Snake outsmarts and outfights any minion fool enough to mistake his blindness for weakness.

Failure to please King Snake cost Lynx an eye

NOCTURNA

Laser radiation drained Natalia Knight's skin of all pigment and rendered her sensitive to sunlight, an accident not entirely unfortunate for an astronomer romantically drawn to twilight. From dusk 'til dawn, Natalia's alter-ego Nocturna and her foster-brother Anton Knight engaged in thievery to enjoy the witching hour's luxuries. But when Anton became the murderous Night-Slayer, Nocturna killed him and turned her attentions toward a true defender of the dark… Batman!

MAXIE ZEUS

Possessing a "god complex" like no other, Maxie Zeus believes himself to be the returned incarnation of Zeus, the mythical Greek ruler of the heavens. Maxie once ruled over a significant portion of Gotham's criminal realm, establishing his own version of Olympus along mythological lines.

BLACK MASK

Janus Cosmetics heir Roman Sionis harbors a bizarre fascination with masks, a fixation that resulted in financial ruin when his company marketed a line of ill-conceived, toxic "Facepaint." When WayneCorp bailed out the floundering company, Sionis resigned in humiliation. Later, he carved a death-mask from the lid of his late father's ebony coffin and established the "False Face Society of Gotham," a gang of masquerading thugs with Sionis as its "Black Mask" figurehead. Once dominating Gotham's underworld, Black Mask's grip was weakened by No Man's Land, though he schemes a return to power.

GENERAL McGOG

Supreme commander of the Trojan Army – a legion of elite mercenaries – General Horatio McGog sentenced Jean Paul Valley to death when the Agent of the Bat entered the Trojans' secret Middle Eastern camp in search of his true origins. But McGog denied Jean Paul the answers he sought, shooting a woman who may have been Azrael's birth-mother. The truth died with her as she leapt into McGog's line of fire in order to save Jean Paul's life.

KING SNAKE

International crime lord Sir Edmund Dorrance hates Robin with a blind rage. His first battle with Tim Drake ended in King Snake's defeat and a loss of face with the Ghost Dragons, his former gang of street punks, now led by the lovely Lynx. In their last meeting, Robin foiled Dorrance's attempt to seize leadership of the criminal Kobra cult. Dorrance was plotting to restore his eyesight using a healing Lazarus Pit under Kobra's control. But in a pitched battle, Robin accidentally spilled cobra venom in the raging King Snake's eyes, undoing the Pit's healing work!

BLACKGATE

HARD TIME is the only time served in Blackgate Island Maximum Security Penitentiary. Formerly a Civil War gun battery defending Gotham Harbor from Confederate Ironsides, the stone fortress of Blackgate later found new purpose in keeping Gotham City's criminal populace at a safe distance. Just a few degrees southeast of the sandy Chalfont Shoal, Blackgate is separated from the larger Gotham Island by "The Rip," a 30-knot current even more intimidating than the northerly swimming sharks basking offshore. Home to an incendiary mix of Gotham's deadliest felons, Blackgate resides in infamy as perhaps the most dangerous prison in America, if not the world!

MAXIMUM SECURITY
Built upon 70 acres of rock in Gotham Bay, Blackgate's cells are reserved for Gotham's "highest risk" prisoners; lesser offenders are sent to upstate facilities.

THE RATCATCHER
Otis Flannegan plagued Gotham with an army of trained rats. Despite his incarceration, the Ratcatcher utilizes a brood of loyal rodents to relay messages to other convicts via the maze of ventilation ducts within Blackgate's superstructure.

Ground-level tier: Death Row… "Closest to Hell"

5-ft outer wall of steel-reinforced concrete

HIGH TIDE!

Rocked to its foundations by Gotham's earthquake, Blackgate weathered even harsher aftershocks in the hours that followed, including a series of 10 seismic-generated tsunamis led by a tidal wave cresting nearly 80 feet!

PROS AND CONS

With a population topping 2,000 inmates, Blackgate's charges are watched over by a force of only 200 corrections officers – unsettling odds considering the significant ratio of dangerous costumed criminals incarcerated among them.

STEELJACKET (real name unknown)

Genetically-altered killer who wears an armored flight-suit to protect his fragile, bird-like bones.

KGBEAST (aka Anatoly Kniazev)

Russian assassin serving life for murder and terrorism.

BLACK SPIDER (aka Johnny LaMonica)

Former enforcer in the employ of Gotham's notorious Black Mask Gang.

CLUEMASTER (aka Arthur Brown)

Mastermind once compelled to leave clues revealing his impending crimes.

KGBeast, the Trigger Twins, and Lock-Up prowl their prison island empire.

WHO WATCHES THE WATCHMEN?

Abandoned by its keepers, the Blackgate of No Man's Land was governed by its own prisoners! Sanctioned by Batman, Lock-Up (Lyle Bolton) meted out punishments with KGBeast and the Trigger Twins (Tad and Tom) until Batman sent Nightwing to restore order.

BATMAN'S CAREER

FOR DC COMICS' Dark Knight Detective, the leap from pulp fiction protagonist to literary icon was accomplished in a handful of decades. Creator Bob Kane's vision of an urban guerrilla clad in the night itself burst his way out of a genre peopled with all manner of costumed mystery men and women, each drawing a line against crime gone unchecked. But the cape and cowl of Batman overshadowed many of his vigilante peers, enduring in popularity for more than 60 years and counting, spanning the 20th century's surrender to a new century and millennium. Today, the Dark Knight and his supporting cast belong to the collective consciousness, a mass media phenomenon borne out of well over 3,000 comic book appearances read, shared, and enjoyed by fans of every demographic in more than 50 countries where "hero" can also be defined by the silhouette of a bat.

Batman Timeline

Since 1939 the Caped Crusader has patrolled Gotham City with tireless vigor. And while the overall look and feel of Batman and his beloved Gotham may have changed with time, the story remains fundamentally unchanged: The Dark Knight and his loyal allies will not rest as long as criminals reign in HIS city!

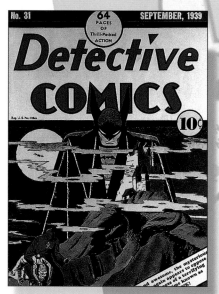

Batman's vampiric influences were first explored in his epic conflict with the undead Monk.

1939

May: **Batman** makes his debut. His ally **Commissioner James Gordon** also appears. (DETECTIVE COMICS #27)

July: **Dr. Death** debuts as the first recurring Bat-villain. Batman's **Utility Belt** is also first spotlighted. (DETECTIVE COMICS #29)

September: Bruce Wayne's fiancée, actress **Julie Madison**, is introduced as the Batman encounters **The Monk**, a werewolf-vampire. The **Bat-Gyro**, a precursor to the Bat-Plane, and the **Batarang** are also first seen. (DETECTIVE COMICS #31)

October: To end The Monk's reign of terror, Batman destroys him and his ally **Dala** by shooting them with silver bullets! (DETECTIVE COMICS #32)

November: In "The Batman and How He Came to Be," the murders of **Thomas and Martha Wayne** are recounted. (DETECTIVE COMICS #33)

1940

February: Batman matches wits with the evil **Professor Hugo Strange**. (DETECTIVE COMICS #36)

March: Batman dons night-vision goggles. (DETECTIVE COMICS #37)

April: After his trapeze-artist parents are slain by gangster **Boss Zucco**, Dick Grayson joins the Dark Knight's crime-fighting crusade as **Robin the Boy Wonder**. (DETECTIVE COMICS #38)

Spring: **The Joker** and **Catwoman** (referred to as "The Cat") debut with the launch of BATMAN, the Caped Crusader's own title. A **Bat-plane** armed with a machine gun is also unveiled. In another tale, Batman guns down the giants of Hugo Strange; hereafter, Batman rejects the use of firearms. (BATMAN #1)

June: Thespian Basil Karlo takes on the role of serial murderer **Clayface**. (DETECTIVE COMICS #40)

July: Robin tackles his first solo adventure. Nevertheless, Batman aids the Boy Wonder in wrapping up the case. (DETECTIVE COMICS #41)

The Penguin made his first Bat-cover appearance in September, 1942.

Fall: **Catwoman** first appears in costume. (BATMAN #3) Batman shares top-billing with Superman in the debut of WORLD'S BEST COMICS, soon to become WORLD'S FINEST COMICS with publication of its second issue. (WORLD'S BEST COMICS #1)

1941

Winter: Batman's home **Gotham City** is first named. (BATMAN #4)

February: Hinting at the Batcave to come, the Dynamic Duo race through a secret tunnel beneath **Wayne Manor** to a barn concealing Batman's roadster, referred to as "**The Batmobile.**" (DETECTIVE COMICS #48)

March: Julie Madison calls off her engagement to Bruce Wayne because of his playboy lifestyle. Using the name Portia Storme, she dons a Robin costume as the Dynamic Duo battle Clayface. (DETECTIVE COMICS #49)

April: Robin acquires his own set of wheels: a pair of rocket-powered roller skates! (DETECTIVE COMICS #50)

Spring: The **Batmobile** roars into action sporting its own bat-headed battering ram. (BATMAN #5)

Summer: Bruce Wayne's latest fling, **Linda Page**, appears. (BATMAN #6)

Fall: The fear-monger **Scarecrow** is introduced. (WORLD'S FINEST COMICS #3)

December: **The Penguin** first waddles into Gotham City. (DETECTIVE COMICS #58)

1942

February: **The Bat-Signal** summons Batman. (DETECTIVE COMICS #60)

August: District Attorney Harvey "Apollo" Kent (later "Dent") and his devilish double **Two-Face** make their debuts. (DETECTIVE COMICS #66)

"Crime's Early Bird" escaped the Dynamic Duo astride a swift ostrich in DETECTIVE COMICS #67.

Less than a year after Batman's debut, a new young hero joined the Dark Knight's crusade.

August–September: A cavern beneath Wayne Manor is revealed as Batman's "secret underground hangars." (BATMAN #12)

1943

April: Rogues **Tweedledee and Tweedledum** appear. (DETECTIVE COMICS #74)

April–May: **Alfred** is introduced as the Wayne family valet. (BATMAN #16)

November: Batman and Robin encounter the swashbuckling **Cavalier**. (DETECTIVE COMICS #81)

1944

January: Batman's underground lair is called "The Bat Cave." (DETECTIVE COMICS #83)

August–September: Batman and Robin journey to ancient Rome in their first time-travel adventure. (BATMAN #24)

October–November: In the first major Bat-villain team-up, the Joker and Penguin join forces to thwart the Caped Crusader! (BATMAN #25)

1945

December 1944–January: The **Bat-Sled** enables the Dynamic Duo and Alfred to enjoy a little winter fun. (BATMAN #26)

1946

April: Scotland Yard provides Batman and Robin with the first official **Bat-Boat** to speed their search for the evil **Professor Moriarty**. (DETECTIVE COMICS #110)

June–July: A blonde Catwoman appears in a prototype of her classic purple cat-eared costume. (BATMAN #35)

1947

June–July: Aliens appear for the first time on a Batman comic book cover. (BATMAN #41)

1948

June-July: The detailed origin of Batman is published. In this tale, the Dark Knight tracks down **Joe Chill**, the gunman who murdered his parents! (BATMAN #47)

October: **The Riddler** begins his career of criminal conundrums. (DETECTIVE COMICS #140)

October-November: **The Mad Hatter** hangs his chapeau in Batman's rogues gallery. Photographer **Vicki Vale**, the Dark Knight's most enduring love-interest (1948 to 1962), is introduced. (BATMAN #49)

1949

May: Batman and Robin employ a "Sub-Batmarine" to net the **Tiger Shark**. (DETECTIVE COMICS #147)

1950

February: After the Batmobile is totaled, Batman and Robin design a new model with bat-headed grille. (DETECTIVE COMICS #156)

June–July: **Deadshot** takes aim at the Dark Knight. (BATMAN #59)

October–November: **Batplane II** is revealed as Batman and Robin enter the Jet Age. (BATMAN #61)

1951

December 1950–January: Catwoman's origin is chronicled. (BATMAN #62)

February: In "The Man Behind the Red Hood," the Joker's origin is revealed. (DETECTIVE COMICS #168)

February–March: **Killer Moth**'s debut ends in defeat. (BATMAN #63)

1952

June: Batman and Robin fight **The Firefly**. (DETECTIVE COMICS #184)

July–August: Batman and **Superman** finally meet, heralding the most enduring super-hero friendship of all time. (SUPERMAN #76)

August: The **Flying Batcave** takes to the air. (DETECTIVE COMICS #186)

1953

February–March: Batman grapples with "The Gorilla Boss of Gotham City," BATMAN's first ape-themed cover. (BATMAN #75)

1954

March: The origin of the Batcave is revealed. (DETECTIVE COMICS #205)

July–August: Batman and Superman begin a series of team-ups in WORLD'S FINEST COMICS lasting most of the title's remaining 32 years. (WORLD'S FINEST COMICS #71)

September: The underwater **Bat-Marine** surfaces. (BATMAN #86)

1955

June: **Ace the Bat-Hound** joins Batman's war on crime (BATMAN #92)

Batman learns that he isn't the first vigilante to make use of the Batcave!

1956

June: The 100th issue of BATMAN is published.

July: Former circus acrobat **Kathy Kane** adds a feminine touch to crime-fighting in Gotham as **Bat-Woman**! (DETECTIVE COMICS #233)

September: The origin of Batman's costume is revealed in a tale featuring Thomas Wayne as the "first" Batman. (DETECTIVE COMICS #235)

1957

September: Diabolical **Professor Milo** renders Batman terrified of bats and briefly forces him to adopt a new identity: "Starman." (DETECTIVE COMICS #247)

December: **The Signal-Man** makes his first appearance. (BATMAN #112)

1958

March: **The Terrible Trio** (The Fox, The Shark, and The Vulture) tussle with Batman and Robin. (DETECTIVE COMICS #253)

Mogo the Bat-Ape joins the Bat-Family. (BATMAN #114)

April: Batman adds the **Bat-Copter** to his vehicle fleet. (DETECTIVE COMICS #254)

July: **Whirly-Bats** – personal mini-copters – are deployed by the Dynamic Duo. (DETECTIVE COMICS #257)

September: **The Calendar Man** challenges Batman. (DETECTIVE COMICS #259)

November: Batman and Robin grapple with the amazing **Dr. Double X**. (DETECTIVE COMICS #261)

1959

February: **Mr. Zero** chills the Caped Crusader. In subsequent appearances, Zero is known by the now-familiar name **Mr. Freeze**. (BATMAN #121)

May: Batman meets the inter-dimensional imp **Bat-Mite**. (DETECTIVE COMICS #267)

1960

April: A married Batman and Batwoman appear in an imaginary tale that features their son as Robin, while an adult Dick Grayson assumes the role of Dark Knight Detective! (BATMAN #131)

March: To defeat alien starfish **Starro the Conqueror**, Batman teams with Wonder Woman, Superman, The Flash, Green Lantern, and The Martian Manhunter to form **The Justice League of America**. The JLA soon graduate to their own series with Batman a frequent member. (THE BRAVE AND THE BOLD #28)

1961

April: Kathy Kane's niece Bette joins the Bat-Family as a blonde **Bat-Girl**. (BATMAN #139)

December: Matt Hagen becomes the monstrously malleable **Clayface II**. (DETECTIVE COMICS #298)

1962

May: In a tale declared "The Story of the Year!" on its cover, Batman becomes a **Bat-Baby**! (BATMAN #147)

Inspired by the Dark Knight, Barbara Gordon fights crime as Batgirl!

1963

January: **The Cat-Man** takes a swipe at the Dynamic Duo. (DETECTIVE COMICS #311)

1964

May: Batman's "new look" premiers. His comic-book costume now mirrors the television Caped Crusader's. (DETECTIVE COMICS #327)

June: Alfred is "killed off" for a short spell. (DETECTIVE COMICS #328)

June–July: Robin forms **The Teen Titans** with super-hero "sidekicks" Kid Flash and Aqualad. (THE BRAVE AND THE BOLD #54)

In their very first meeting, Batman caught the thieving Catwoman, but remarkably allowed her to escape!

December: The otherworldly menace **The Outsider** appears. (DETECTIVE COMICS #334)

1965

November: The Duo encounter Mark Desmond, aka **Blockbuster**. (DETECTIVE COMICS #345)

1966

January–February: Robin and his Teen Titan pals (now including Wonder Girl) matriculate to their own comic book. (TEEN TITANS #1)

May: **Cluemaster** confounds Batman. (DETECTIVE COMICS #351)

June: The alluring **Poison Ivy** plants her first toxic kiss. (BATMAN #181)

August: Batman meets the hypnotic Asian crimelord **Dr. Tzin-Tzin**. (DETECTIVE COMICS #354)

October: Alfred returns to Wayne Manor, restored to normalcy after he is revealed to be the evil Outsider. (DETECTIVE COMICS #356)

December: **Spellbinder I** turns Batman's world upside-down. (DETECTIVE COMICS #358)

1967

January: Barbara Gordon dons cape and cowl as **Batgirl**. (DETECTIVE COMICS #359)

October–November: Batman joins forces with the **Metal Men** in the pages of THE BRAVE AND THE BOLD. The title teamed the Caped Crusader with a host of DC super-heroes until its cancellation at issue #200 in 1983. (THE BRAVE AND THE BOLD #74)

1968

January: The *Batman* TV series' Batmobile briefly becomes the official comic-book Bat-vehicle. (DETECTIVE COMICS #371)

March: To celebrate the bicentennial issue of his self-titled series, Batman battles the Scarecrow in "The Man Who Radiated Fear." (BATMAN #200)

1969

May: Batman celebrates his 30th anniversary in DETECTIVE COMICS. (DETECTIVE COMICS #387)

October: Private Investigator **Jason Bard** – ally to the Bat-Family, partner to Man-Bat, and later love interest for Barbara Gordon – is introduced. (DETECTIVE COMICS #392)

December: In "One Bullet Too Many," Dick Grayson leaves the Batcave for Hudson University. Bruce Wayne and Alfred decamp to the penthouse of the Wayne Foundation building. A new Batcave is established beneath the WF skyscraper. (BATMAN #217)

Batman abandons his previous Batmobile for a turbo-charged sports car. (DETECTIVE COMICS #394)

1970

January: The camp hi-jinks of the past two decades' Bat-tales end as writer Dennis O'Neil and artist Neal Adams revitalize the Dark Knight, establishing the present-day tone and mood of the series. (DETECTIVE COMICS #395)

June: Zoologist Kirk Langstrom transforms into **Man-Bat**, to the horror of his fiancée Francine Lee. Also, Robin and Batgirl team up for the first time. (DETECTIVE COMICS #400)

November: After debuting in the pages of STRANGE ADVENTURES #215, **The League of Assassins** first appears in a Bat-title. (DETECTIVE COMICS #405)

1971

January: In "Marriage: Impossible," Kirk Langstrom's bride Francine Lee Langstrom becomes **She-Bat**. (DETECTIVE COMICS #407)

May: Beautiful-but-deadly **Talia** appears, predating the debut of her diabolical father, **Rā's al Ghūl**. (DETECTIVE COMICS #411)

June: Rā's al Ghūl proves himself to be Batman's most formidable foe. (BATMAN #232)

1972

August: On the cover of his 400th appearance in DETECTIVE COMICS, Batman holds a gun to his temple, having written a suicide note to Robin, Batgirl, and Superman! (DETECTIVE COMICS #426)

1973

April: **The Spook** makes a chilling debut. (DETECTIVE COMICS #434)

1974

October–November: Batman joins forces with **Manhunter** Paul Kirk for the only time when Kirk sacrifices his life to destroy the evil cabal known as the Council. (DETECTIVE COMICS #443)

Even while transformed into Man-Bat, Kirk Langstrom was determined to hear wedding bells!

1975

April–May: The debut of RICHARD DRAGON: KUNG-FU FIGHTER features the title character and Ben Turner (aka **Bronze Tiger**), martial artists who will cross paths with the Bat-Family.

May: Batman's arch-foe appears in his own series of misadventures with THE JOKER, a monthly series lasting only nine issues. (THE JOKER #1)

September–October: THE BATMAN FAMILY, a series spotlighting the cast of Bat-characters, debuts. 20 issues will be published before cancellation in 1978. (THE BATMAN FAMILY #1)

1976

December 1975–January: Man-Bat flies solo in his own monthly adventures, lasting just two issues. (MAN-BAT #1)

The 1950 Batmobile was just the first of many sophisticated crime-fighting cruisers. The Dynamic Duo built this model themselves, outfitting it with a knife-edged battering ram!

January: **Lady Shiva**, both friend and foe to the Bat-Family in later years, is introduced. (RICHARD DRAGON, KUNG-FU FIGHTER #5)

February–March: Cult leader **Kobra**, soon to be a frequent foe of Batman, appears in his own series. (KOBRA #1)

March: Kindly **Dr. Leslie Thompkins**, who befriends young Bruce Wayne, debuts in "There Is No Hope In Crime Alley." (DETECTIVE COMICS #457)

June: Pirate rogue **Captain Stingaree** appears. (DETECTIVE COMICS #460)

September: Batman battles **Black Spider**. (DETECTIVE COMICS #463)

1977

May: **Dr. Phosphorus** makes a fiery debut. (DETECTIVE COMICS #469)

June: Platinum bombshell **Silver St. Cloud** is introduced as Bruce Wayne's latest short-lived romantic interest. (DETECTIVE COMICS #470)

1978

April–May: **Rebecca "Becky" Langstrom**, baby daughter of Kirk and Francine Langstrom, is born. (THE BATMAN FAMILY #17)

July–August: Acromegalic Preston Payne melts into the role of **Clayface III**. (DETECTIVE COMICS #478)

1979

January: **Lucius Fox** is introduced as the financial wizard guiding Wayne Enterprises' day-to-day business operations in Bruce Wayne's absence. (BATMAN #307)

April–May: In the 40th anniversary issue of DETECTIVE COMICS, gangster **Maxie Zeus** appears. (DETECTIVE COMICS #483)

August–September: Kathy Kane is murdered by the Bronze Tiger. (DETECTIVE COMICS #485)

October: The pyromaniac **Firebug** flames alight. (BATMAN #318)

1980

July: UNTOLD LEGENDS OF THE BATMAN, the first Batman mini-series, premieres.

August: **Arkham Asylum** is introduced. (BATMAN #326)

September: **The Crime Doctor** prescribes death for the Dark Knight! (DETECTIVE COMICS #494)

October: In a preview tale, Robin is joined by former Teen Titans Wonder Girl and Kid Flash, as well as new members Changeling, Raven, Cyborg, and Starfire to form **The New Teen Titans**. (DC COMICS PRESENTS #26)

1981

January: **The Electrocutioner** makes his shocking debut. (BATMAN #331)

March: In "To Kill a Legend," the 500th issue of DETECTIVE COMICS, Batman and Robin visit an alternate reality where they prevent the murders of Thomas and Martha Wayne.

1982

February: The illusory villain **Mirage** debuts. (DETECTIVE COMICS #511)

March: DETECTIVE COMICS marks its 45th anniversary with the return of **Dr. Death**. (DETECTIVE COMICS #512)

October: The Dark Knight battles **Colonel Blimp**. (BATMAN #352)

1983

March: As young circus acrobat **Jason Todd** makes his first appearance, **Killer Croc** begins a run of reptilian villainy. (BATMAN #357)

May: The Dark Knight celebrates his 500th appearance in DETECTIVE COMICS. Mirroring Dick Grayson's own origins, the murders of Jason Todd's circus aerialist parents by Killer Croc lead to Jason inheriting the mantle of Robin from Dick. (DETECTIVE COMICS #526)

July: Slovenly Gotham cop with a heart of gold **Harvey Bullock** is introduced. (BATMAN #361)

August: Batman quits the Justice League of America and assembles his own team of super-heroes, **The Outsiders**, in a new comic book series. (BATMAN AND THE OUTSIDERS #1)

Siblings Anton and Natalia Knight – aka **Night-Slayer** and **Nocturna** – debut. (DETECTIVE COMICS #529)

During their many duels, Batman tested his mettle against the Cavalier's deadly épée!

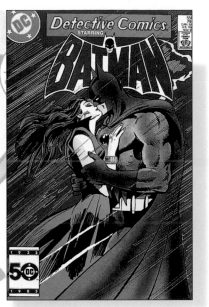

Nocturna once thought she could charm the Batman into becoming her midnight mate!

December: Jason Todd officially debuts as Robin. (BATMAN #366)

1984

February: Dick Grayson quits the role of Robin. (THE NEW TEEN TITANS #39)

July: Dick Grayson dons the guise of **Nightwing** to rescue his fellow Titans from **Deathstroke the Terminator** and **The HIVE**. (TALES OF THE TEEN TITANS #44)

1985

April: DC Comics' CRISIS ON INFINITE EARTHS begins. During this 12-issue series Batman's history is radically altered. Bat-Mite, Ace the Bat-Hound, and other Bat-characters are forgotten. Jason Todd's origin story is revised, leading to a less likable version of the character.

August: Crimelord Roman Sionis, alias **Black Mask**, appears. (BATMAN #386)

1986

March: Writer/artist Frank Miller's BATMAN: THE DARK KNIGHT RETURNS, is published. The four-issue mini-series becomes one of the best-selling and most celebrated Batman stories in the character's history.

October: The 400th issue of BATMAN is published.

1987

February: Frank Miller and artist David Mazzucchelli's four-part "Batman: Year One" redefines the early days of Bruce Wayne's crime-fighting career. (BATMAN #404-407)

March: One of the longest-running comic-book series, DETECTIVE COMICS celebrates its 50th anniversary. On the cover, Batman matches sleuthing skills with **Sherlock Holmes**! (DETECTIVE COMICS #572)

Detective Sarah Essen, later police commissioner and wife of James Gordon, appears as "Batman: Year One" continues. (BATMAN #405)

June: Jason Todd makes his debut post-CRISIS appearance as a troubled orphan of Crime Alley. (BATMAN #408)

"Batman: Year Two" introduces **The Reaper** and reaffirms Bruce Wayne's vow to never take up firearms in his crusade. (DETECTIVE COMICS #575)

August: Kobra creates **Lady Clayface**. (THE OUTSIDERS vol. 1 #21)

October: Batman meets the malevolent **Mime**. (BATMAN #412)

In the graphic novel BATMAN: SON OF THE DEMON, the Dark Knight and Talia's affair leads to the birth of a son. Their relationship ends before Batman learns of his child. Batman's son is never mentioned again in continuity.

1988

February: **The Ventriloquist and Scarface** begin their partnership. (DETECTIVE COMICS #583)

March: **The KGBeast** ignites a cold war. (BATMAN #417)

April: **The Ratcatcher** embarks on a verminous criminal career. (DETECTIVE COMICS #585)

November: Madman **Cornelius Stirk** debuts. (DETECTIVE COMICS #592)

December: The "A Death in the Family" storyline begins. (BATMAN #426)

BATMAN: THE KILLING JOKE offers a new twist on the Clown Prince of Crime and his beginnings. The Joker shoots and paralyzes Barbara Gordon.

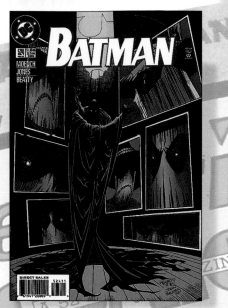

For over 60 years, the Joker has concocted a myriad murder scenarios for the Dark Knight!

Barbara Gordon's final adventure as Batgirl is chronicled in her first-ever solo book. (BATGIRL SPECIAL #1)

1989

February: As "A Death in the Family" draws to its catastrophic conclusion, Bat-fans vote to decide Jason Todd's fate. By a slim margin, readers decree that Jason should perish, and he dies at the hands of the Joker. (BATMAN #428)

Catwoman sinks her claws into her own four-issue mini-series. (CATWOMAN #1)

April: The **Huntress** – soon to bring her unique brand of justice to Gotham – debuts in her own monthly series. (THE HUNTRESS #1)

Roland Desmond, brother of the late Mark Desmond, mutates into an all-new Blockbuster. (STARMAN #9)

May: The 600th issue of DETECTIVE COMICS is published, concluding the three-part "Blind Justice" by *Batman* movie co-screenwriter Sam Hamm.

August: **Tim Drake** makes his first appearance as the four-part "Batman: Year Three" begins. (BATMAN #436)

September: The surviving Clayfaces unite as **The Mudpack**, part of Basil Karlo's scheme to usurp their powers as **The Ultimate Clayface**! (DETECTIVE COMICS #604)

November: Billed as "The first new 'solo' Batman book since 1940," BATMAN: LEGENDS OF THE DARK KNIGHT is published, exploring stories outside established Bat-continuity.

Gotham sees a new masked vigilante: teenager Lonnie Machin's authority-antagonizing **Anarky**. (DETECTIVE COMICS #608)

December: Tim Drake's first official appearance highlights "A Lonely Place of Dying," a five-part epic leading to Tim Drake's debut as the new Robin. (BATMAN #440-#442, THE NEW TITANS #60-61)

BATMAN: GOTHAM BY GASLIGHT becomes the first of many "Elseworlds", featuring the Dark Knight re-imagined across time and space.

1990

February: Barbara Gordon takes the role of all-seeing information broker **Oracle**. (SUICIDE SQUAD #38)

May: The mute engineer-savant **Harold** makes his debut as one of the Penguin's henchmen. (BATMAN #447)

July: The voodoo chieftain **Obeah Man** is introduced in a tale leading to the death of Tim Drake's mother. (DETECTIVE COMICS #618)

November: In the first of three mini-series chronicling the new Robin's adventures, Tim Drake defeats British crimelord Sir Edmund Dorrance, aka **King Snake**. (ROBIN vol. 1 #1)

December: Tim Drake officially joins Batman's crusade as the third Robin. (BATMAN #457)

1991

January: Harold makes his home in the Batcave as mechanic-in-residence. (BATMAN #458)

February: The evil **Abbatoir** appears. (DETECTIVE COMICS #625)

October: Tim Drake's second mini-series pits the new Boy Wonder against the Clown Prince of Crime! (ROBIN II: THE JOKER'S WILD! #1)

1992

May: Gotham police officer **Renee Montoya** makes her debut.

The electrically-challenged **Galvan** debuts. (DETECTIVE COMICS #644)

June: The Dark Knight's adventures are unveiled in a new monthly title, BATMAN: SHADOW OF THE BAT, published over eight years and 93 issues. Arkham administrator **Jeremiah Arkham** and serial killer **Mr. Zsasz** appear in the first issue.

August: Stephanie Brown, aka **The Spoiler**, becomes a vigilante to thwart her father, **Cluemaster**. (DETECTIVE COMICS #647)

The Scarecrow remains one of Batman's most frightening foes.

Hulking man-child **Amygdala** also debuts this month. (BATMAN: SHADOW OF THE BAT #3)

October: Jean Paul Valley and his alter-ego, the avenging angel **Azrael**, appear. (BATMAN: SWORD OF AZRAEL #1)

December: Robin's third mini-series teams him with Huntress. (ROBIN III: CRY OF THE HUNTRESS #1)

1993

January: **Bane** smashes into Bat-history. (BATMAN: VENGEANCE OF BANE #1)

Ulysses Hadrian Armstrong causes trouble as **The General**. (DETECTIVE COMICS #654)

February: The multi-part "Knightfall" begins as Bane sets out to destroy Batman. (BATMAN #492)

July: As "Knightfall" continues, Bane breaks Batman's back, paralyzing him. Bruce relinquishes the mantle of the bat to Jean Paul Valley for a brief and tumultuous time. (BATMAN #497)

August: The tales of femme fatale and reluctant do-gooder Catwoman are told in her own series. (CATWOMAN #1)

September: The mentally-unbalanced **Tally Man** appears. (BATMAN: SHADOW OF THE BAT #19)

October: Jean Paul Valley adopts more formidable Bat-armor to defeat Bane. (BATMAN #500)

The Trigger Twins make their debut. (DETECTIVE COMICS #663)

November: Robin's own ongoing series launches. (ROBIN vol. 2 #1)

1994

June: The Huntress returns to stalk criminal prey in a four-issue mini-series. (THE HUNTRESS vol. 2 #1)

July: In "KnightsEnd," Bruce Wayne battles to reclaim the mantle of the bat from the maddened Jean Paul Valley. (BATMAN #509)

August: As "KnightsEnd" ends, Jean Paul Valley returns the guise of Batman to Bruce Wayne. (BATMAN: LEGENDS OF THE DARK KNIGHT #63)

October: Batman's origins are recounted in zero-numbered editions of his four flagship titles. In this revised history, he never discovers the identity of his parents' murderer. (BATMAN #0, DETECTIVE COMICS #0, BATMAN: SHADOW OF THE BAT #0, BATMAN: LEGENDS OF THE DARK KNIGHT #0)

November: The multi-part "Prodigal" begins as Dick Grayson assumes the role of Batman while Bruce Wayne attends to a secret agenda. (BATMAN #512)

1995

January: As "Prodigal" concludes, Bruce Wayne once more takes up cape and cowl as the Dark Knight. (ROBIN #13)

MacKenzie "Hardback" Bock joins the Gotham police force as Batman first encounters the bloodthirsty **Steeljacket**. (DETECTIVE COMICS #681)

February: Jean Paul Valley begins an odyssey to discover his true place in the world with the launch of Azrael's own ongoing series. (AZRAEL #1)

The deadly **Silver Monkey** appears. (DETECTIVE COMICS #685)

July: THE BATMAN CHRONICLES debuts. This quarterly anthology lasts 23 issues and touch all facets of the Dark Knight, his allies, and his rogues gallery.

Modern-day privateer **Cap'n Fear** appears. (DETECTIVE COMICS #687)

September: Dick Grayson makes his solo debut with a four-issue mini-series. (NIGHTWING #1)

October: **Firebug II** sets Gotham ablaze. (DETECTIVE COMICS #690)

November: Perennial loser Killer Moth forsakes his soul to become the insectoid monster **Charaxes**. (UNDERWORLD UNLEASHED #1)

Spellbinder II makes her debut. (DETECTIVE COMICS #691)

December: Incarceration expert **Lock-Up** inflicts his own brand of justice on Gotham's criminals. (ROBIN #23)

1996

January: **The Allergent** targets Gotham's flora, making enemies of Poison Ivy and Batman. (DETECTIVE COMICS #693)

February: The schizoid **Schism** makes his debut. (BATMAN #527)

March: The epic "Contagion" begins. Hundreds of thousands die as the Ebola Gulf-A virus ("The Clench") is loosed upon Gotham. (BATMAN: SHADOW OF THE BAT #48)

April: "Baby-Bat" Aaron Langstrom, the son of Kirk and Francine Langstrom appears. (MAN-BAT #3)

May: The nefarious **Narcosis** first appears. (BATMAN: SHADOW OF THE BAT #50)

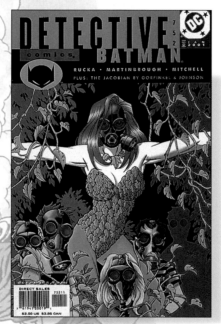

Since 1966, "flora fatale" Poison Ivy has grown wild in Gotham City.

August: Batman races to stop Rā's al Ghūl from unleashing yet another plague as the multi-part "Legacy" concludes in the 700th issue of DETECTIVE COMICS.

October: Dick Grayson graduates to his own monthly adventures with the launch of the NIGHTWING series.

The Ogre and **Ape** make their debuts. (BATMAN #535)

December: Commissioner James Gordon appears in his first solo mini-series. (BATMAN: GORDON'S LAW #1)

The "Elseworlds" KINGDOM COME offers a glimpse of a troubled future for Batman. (KINGDOM COME #1-4)

1997

March: Bruce Wayne's latest flame, radio host Vesper Fairchild, makes her first appearance. (BATMAN #540)

May: Anarky stars in his own four-issue mini-series. (ANARKY vol. 1 #1)

November: In the centennial issue of BATMAN: LEGENDS OF THE DARK KNIGHT, Dick Grayson's origin as Robin is retold, while Jason Todd's Boy Wonder is given a final farewell.

The origin of Mr. Freeze is finally revealed. (BATMAN: MR. FREEZE)

1998

January: **Cassius,** the fifth Clayface, debuts. (BATMAN #550)

Kidnapper Nathan Finch returns with robotic prosthetics and a thirst for vengeance as **Gearhead**! (DETECTIVE COMICS #717)

April: Gotham City is devastated by an earthquake, beginning the "Cataclysm" tale. (BATMAN: SHADOW OF THE BAT #73)

July: The killer **Brutale** appears (NIGHTWING #22)

October: Bat-rogues **Ferak** and **The Answer** appear. (BATMAN VILLAINS SECRET FILES #1)

Azrael's ties to the Batcave are re-established, resulting in a title change to his series. The evil **Nicholas Scratch** debuts. (AZRAEL: AGENT OF THE BAT #47)

1999

January: Barbara Gordon (as Oracle) appears in her own monthly series, joining forces with **Black Canary**. (BIRDS OF PREY #1)

March: "No Man's Land" begins. Gotham is now made up of fiefdoms ruled by escaped Bat-rogues. (BATMAN: NO MAN'S LAND #1)

As Gotham disintegrates, Nightwing joins a regrouped and older Titans. (THE TITANS #1)

May: Anarky stars in his own series, lasting eight issues. (ANARKY vol. 2 #1)

July: Martial arts prodigy **Cassandra Cain**, inheritor of the mantle of Batgirl, makes her appearance. The assassin **Cain** also debuts. (BATMAN #567)

Covert agent **Echo** appears. (LEGENDS OF THE DARK KNIGHT #119)

October: **Harley Quinn** makes her official Bat-continuity comics debut from *Batman: The Animated Series*. (BATMAN: HARLEY QUINN #1)

2000

January: After a year of "No Man's Land," Metropolis mogul Lex Luthor spearheads the rebuilding of Gotham City. (BATMAN #573)

February: The Joker murders James Gordon's wife, Sarah Essen-Gordon, in "Endgame," the penultimate chapter of "No Man's Land." (DETECTIVE COMICS #741)

March: BATMAN: GOTHAM KNIGHTS is launched, featuring back-up black-and-white stories from some of the comics' most illustrious creators.

Patriotic zealot **The Banner** threatens the stability of a rebuilt Gotham. (BATMAN #575)

April: The new adventures of Batgirl begin with the publication of her own ongoing series. (BATGIRL #1)

Kyle Abbot and **Whisper A'Daire**, agents of Rā's al Ghūl, appear. (DETECTIVE COMICS #743)

May: Batman encounters the undead spirit **Samsara**. (BATMAN: GOTHAM KNIGHTS #3)

July: The Dark Knight battles **Orca**. (BATMAN #579)

November: Rā's al Ghūl and Batman face one another yet again as DETECTIVE COMICS celebrates 750 issues!

The Dark Knight continues the good fight into the 21st century!

IMAGINARY WORLDS

HIS PASSION FOR JUSTICE is not limited merely to Gotham City in the here and now – the Dark Knight's adventures span myriad realms. In "Elseworlds" as divergent as night is to day, Batman lives on in less familiar guises, fighting crime and injustice in parallel realities. Some are settings all too familiar, but with an ironic and unsuspecting twist. Others are cut from the ephemeral fabric of dreams… or *nightmares*. And still others are eras and places that cannot, could not, or perhaps *should not* exist. In this multiverse of alternate worlds, the one constant is a boy named Bruce whose destiny as a hero molded in the image of a bat transcends both time and space.

SIR BRUCE
To avenge the murders of his beloved parents, the Lord and Lady of the House of Waynesmoor, young Bruce would slay the enchantress Morgana Le Fay!

THREE TALES IN TIME

Consider these three generations of Batman: The Dark Knight of Arthur Pendragon's Round Table vowed his liege lord's destruction, but crusaded bravely against the infidel hordes of Rā's al Ghūl; the Batman of a mirror universe was astounded to learn that Dracula was indeed real, alive, and well in present-day Gotham; while barely a century removed in time but another world away, a 19th-century Bat-Man stalked his immortal foes by gaslight!

NOSFERATU
Batman could not strike fear in the undead hearts of Dracula's minions until he became one of them – a bloodthirsty creature of the night!

CLOWN PRINCE OF DARKNESS
Though Dracula was finally destroyed, a few vampires still hunted the Gotham night. The Joker was all too eager to bolster the moldering ranks of night-stalkers, leading them in final conflict against their mutual bane, the Batman!

> I COULDN'T *LIVE* WITHOUT LAUGHTER! HA HA HA HAAA

CAT-WOMAN
Selina Kyle barely survived an encounter with the vampire Creech, who assumed the glamour of a wolf to guzzle her blood. But Creech's teeth had left their mark, piercing Selina's flesh and transforming her by the light of the full moon into a Were-Cat! Selina found brief solace in the arms of the Dark Knight, and with him battled Gotham's horrid vampire mob to her dying breath.

SMILIN' JACK
To satisfy the profane hunger of his unholy master, Mad Jack Schadenfreude found easy pickings among the poor children of "The Devil's Workshop," a squalid corner of Gotham, *circa* 1907.

GUARDIAN OF GOTHAM
Hunter became hunted when Jack's vampiric lord, Baron Montenegro, was pursued by the mysterious "Bat-Man" and master magician Harry Houdini! Together, Gotham's self-appointed protector and the "Ectoplasmic Man" escape artist sent the Baron and his vampiress Leonora back to the Hell that spawned them.

125

Index

Acknowledgments

Dorling Kindersley would like to thank the following
DC artists and writers for their contributions to this book:

Dusty Abell, Neal Adams, Dan Adkins, Charlie Adlard, Quique Alcatena, Pascal Alixe, Murphy Anderson, Jim Aparo, Brian Apthorp, Terry Austin, Michael Bair, Jim Balent, Eduardo Barreto, John Beatty, Scott Beatty, Terry Beatty, J. J. Birch, Bret Blevins, Alex Bleyaert, Brian Bolland, Norm Breyfogle, Pat Broderick, Mat Broome, Eliot Brown, Mark Buckingham, Dennis Budd Jr., Rick Burchett, Ray Burnley, Sal Buscema, Robert Campanella, W.C. Carani, Sergio Cariello, Mark Chiarello, Gene Colan, Mike Collins, Carl Critchlow, Rodolfo Damaggio, Mike DeCarlo, John Dell, Jesse Delperdang, Mike Deodato, Chuck Dixon, Kieron Dwyer, Dale Eaglesham, Steve Englehart, Wayne Faucher, Duncan Fegredo, John Floyd, Gary Frank, Anton Furst, José Luis García-López, Drew Geraci, Joe Giella, Tom Grindberg, Dick Giordano, Michael Golden, Alan Grant, Devin Grayson, Tom Grummett, Butch Guice, Paul Gulacy, Matt Haley, Bob Hall, Scott Hanna, Edward Hannigan, Ian Hannin, Tony Harris, Flint Henry, John Higgins, James Hodgkins, Rob Hunter, Carmine Infantino, Klaus Janson, Phil Jimenez, Dave Johnson,

Staz Johnson, Malcolm Jones III, Kelley Jones, Dan Jurgens, Bob Kane, Sam Kieth, Barry Kitson, Ray Kryssing, Greg Land, Andy Lanning, Bob Layton, Jeph Loeb, Aaron Lopresti, Tom Lyle, Ray McArthy, Scott McDaniel, Bob McLeod, Doug Mahnke, Alex Maleev, Tom Mandrake, Mike Manley, Shawn Martinbrough, Ron Marz, José Marzan Jr., David Mazzucchelli, Mike Mignola, Steve Mitchell, Doug Moench, Sheldon Moldoff, Alan Moore, Win Mortimer, Jeff Moy, Mindy Newell, Don Newton, Tom Nguyen, Graham Nolan, Irv Novick, Dennis O'Neil, Tom Palmer, Jimmy Palmiotti, Sean Parsons, James Pascoe, Jason Pearson, Mark Pennington, Mark Prudeau, Kelley Puckett, Javier Pulido, Jordan Raskin, David Roach, Jerry Robinson, Roger Robinson, Marshall Rogers, William Rosado, Alex Ross, John Royal, Joe Rubinstein, Greg Rucka, P. Craig Russell, Paul Ryan, Tim Sale, Damion Scott, Mike Sellers, Howard Sherman, Bill Sienkiewicz, Bob Smith, Aaron Sowd, Dick Sprang, Jim Starlin, Brian Stelfreeze, Karl Story, Dave Taylor, Frank Teran, Bruce Timm, Chris Warner, Lee Weeks, Mike Wieringo, Anthony Williams, Phil Winslade, Stan Woch, Pete Woods, Patrick Zircher.

The writer would like to thank Jennifer Myskowski and Chuck Dixon for their help in producing this book.
Special thanks also to Matt Idelson, Greg Rucka, Scott Peterson, Graham Nolan, and Mark Waid.

Dorling Kindersley would like to thank the following: Steve Korté, Trent Duffy, Jaye Gardner
at DC Comics; Lisa Lanzarini for design assistance; Hilary Bird for the index.